RAC... ...A TO THE YUKON

Here's to Adventure !

Rod Price

A Lifetime of Adventure Racing from the Everglades to the Amazon to the World's Longest Canoe Race

ROD PRICE

Another Quality Book Published By:
LEGACY BOOK PUBLISHING
1883 Lee Road, Winter Park, FL 32789
www.LEGACYBOOKPUBLISHING.com

Racing to the Yukon

Published by:
LEGACY Book Publishing
1883 Lee Road
Winter Park, Florida 32789
www.LegacyBookPublishing.com

© Rod Price 2010
Printed in the United States
Second Printing
ISBN: 978-1-934449-58-5

Cover Design by Gabriel H. Vaughn

DEDICATION

This book is dedicated to the late Gene Jensen, the father of modern canoe racing, both as a competitor and a master canoe designer. His advice to me personally was, "Rod, don't settle for being mediocre."

I miss you, Gene.

Gene Jensen (left) & Tom Estes (right) - Mpls. Aquatennial Canoe Race (1950)

ACKNOWLEDGEMENTS

I would like to thank all of the people who made this book possible. From race organizers who put together challenging events (often with little financial reward) to rival competitors who forced me to train longer & harder and my teammates who have seen me at my best and at my worst. Thank you for making this adventure packed decade the best one of my life - so far.

Finally, I would like to thank my publisher, Gabriel H. Vaughn. Writing this book was definitely tougher than racing in the Yukon 1000. Thank you for your patience, and help in trying to drag this Neanderthal into the computer age. Your advice and creative touches really make this manuscript sparkle.

TABLE OF CONTENTS

Prologue

Section One

1. Return to the Canoe
2. Everglades Challenge 2003
3. Everglades Challenge 2006
4. Adventure Racing
5. Adirondack Series
   a. 2004
   b. 2005
   c. 2006
   d. 2007
   e. 2008
6. Gator Attack
7. Great Amazon Raft Race
   16 Pages of Color Photos of Section One

Section Two

8. Are you sure you want to do this?
9. Everglades Challenge 2009
10. Atlantic Coast Conquest Adventure Race
11. Thoughts on the Yukon
12. Journey to Whitehorse
13. Day One - Lake LaBerge
14. Day Two - Five Finger Rapids
15. Day Three - Fort Selkirk
16. Day Four - Paddling Across the Border
17. Day Five - Circle, Alaska
18. Day Six - The Flats
19. Day Seven - The Beautiful Bridge
20. Call of the Cheeseburger
21. Epilogue
    16 Pages of Color Photos of Section Two

"There is magic in the feel of a paddle and the movement of a canoe, a magic compounded of distance, adventure, solitude, and peace."

—Sigurd Olson

PROLOGUE

I was seven years old when I participated in my first canoe race in 1967. My father and I were in the YMCA Indian Guides at Camp Waco in Georgia. Our Indian names were Sitting Hawk and Flying Hawk. There were six father-son teams lined-up on the shore of the camp lake. It was a simple course. Paddle out to the middle of the lake, circle a buoy and race back to shore. The event was over in ten minutes, and the Hawk team finished in fourth place. Being a competitive little brat, I blamed my dad for the defeat. In his defense, his sport was baseball. He coached my older brothers and I for years in Little League, and won several titles.

I returned to competitive canoeing in 1980. I heard about a 20 mile canoe race being held on the Oklawaha River in Central Florida. I talked to a friend of mine, Tim Naxsara, into racing with me. Despite only having two practice sessions, we won the race. Since then, the canoe has been a constant part of my life. Whether racing, training or even leisurely paddling down a river, there is an instant feeling of contentment at being on the water in a canoe. It is my connection to nature.

I like the simplicity of the canoe's design. The North American Indians developed the canoe thousands of years ago for traversing the region's rivers and lakes. They spread birch bark over a lightweight, wooden frame, and waterproofed the craft with pine or elm tree resin. Just like our canoes today, they were narrow at each end and wide in the middle for stability. This hydrodynamic design allows the canoe to be propelled through the water with minimal effort.

I often think of my single, racing canoe as a time machine. When I am paddling on a pristine river in Florida, I am seeing virtually the same scenery that the native Timacuans did hundreds of years ago. I try to imagine what their villages would have looked like on the shoreline. I frequently see and hear some of the same wildlife that they encountered. The water birds, alligators, deer and black bears have been in Florida longer than humans.

There is also the tranquility factor that I experience in my canoe. At some point in a lengthy paddling session, my mind seems to separate from the physical toil my body is engaged in. All of the distractions of the hectic, outside world disappear, and I am able to focus my thinking on a particular subject. I sometimes find solutions for problems that have been bothering me for days. After a workout, I feel revitalized and ready to confront the urban world again - knowing that my canoe is always ready and waiting.

I have been asked more than once why I compete in these extreme races. My usual answer is because I enjoy the challenge. That response, however, only begins to explain my reasons. I have come to a point in my thinking where I truly despise the technology that dominates our lives. Is it the goal of our society to eliminate all physical exertion from our lives, and seek continual entertainment for our minds? We have cell phones that play music, send text messages, take pictures and surf the web. When we are not using our phones, we are likely to be in front of the computer or watching our wide-screen, high def. television. And how helpless do we feel when one of these modern conveniences fails? I must admit that although I fight it (don't ever text me), I am as dependent as the next person on our modern appendages. In a world that increasingly demands more accessibility from us, it is nice to occasionally be off-line. When I am competing in a long canoe or adventure race, my world becomes far less complicated. My only concerns are drinking, eating, maybe sleeping and focusing on my performance in the event.

Adventure racing is an escape from the concrete world into the natural world. My business has me driving around a city for hours each day making deliveries. And while I am proud of the company I established 20 years ago, it gets monotonous at times. It is always exciting to travel to new wilderness areas for an adventure race, or paddle down a river for the first time. Very often the beauty of my surroundings has been a welcome distraction from the competition. I have discovered that there is nothing monotonous about nature.

I also enjoy the planning and training that is involved in preparing for a major event. Canoe racing is what I call an "honest" sport. While good paddling technique is important, victory usually goes to the racer who has put in the most time practicing. I like the adage, "If the training is hard, the race will be easy. If the training is easy, the race will be hard."

During the last few years as I have taken on more ambitious challenges, I have begun to wonder if much of our perceived limitations are imagined.

We used to think that running a 26 mile marathon was the ultimate endurance test. Then came the ironman triathlon - a 2.4 mile swim, a 112 mile bike leg followed by a full length marathon. Now there are 50 and 100 mile foot races, and even a triple-ironman triathlon. With the right training program and a positive attitude, there is very little a person cannot do regardless of their age. Studies have shown that athletes in their forties are more mentally equipped to withstand the rigors of an extreme race than their thirty-year old counterparts.

Finally, there is the competitive aspect of extreme racing that satisfies my primal instincts. It has been said that sports are the modern man's warfare. Most of us weekend warriors that participate in extreme sports know that victory is decided by who best combines mental toughness with physical conditioning and a winning strategy. Although I have tremendous respect for my fellow competitors, the real contest involves my own mind and body.

"There comes a time in every race when a competitor meets the real opponent, and understands that it's himself."

—Lance Armstrong

CHAPTER 1

A Return to the Canoe

In December of 1999, I reached forty years of age. Although I was healthy, I was not in athletic shape. I felt okay, but there was definitely something missing from my life. The 1990s had seen a steady decline in my fitness level. Getting married and starting a business shortly before 1990, were two worthy areas to focus my energies on. The birth of my daughter in 1991, was an exciting time. However, the middle 1990s were a stressful period with a divorce and a near bankruptcy. I spent the rest of the decade trying to be a good father, and keeping my business running. I was determined to live the next decade differently. I think being in good physical shape improves your entire outlook on life. My first goal was to get back in shape. I was carrying close to 215 lbs. on my 5' 10" frame. I'm a husky guy to begin with, but this was not muscle. It was "beer belly" weight. I had recently purchased pants with a 38 inch waist for the first time. It was time to take action.

I came across an exercise and diet book that motivated me. It combined strength workouts with cardio sessions. It even prescribed what type of food to eat and how often. I had previously focused on working out without paying attention to what I was eating. The combination of regular gym workouts with limited food consumption was effective. I started dropping pounds immediately, and after a month I was feeling much better.

In February 2000, having lost ten pounds, I drove over to St. Petersburg for a canoe race. I had arranged to borrow a C-1 (one person) racing canoe. In 1990, I was one of the best canoeists in the state. In the late 1980s my partner, Carl Poulsen, and I had traveled all over the state of Florida winning canoe races. From the Panhandle to the Florida Keys we demonstrated our paddling dominance. Armed with this confidence, I thought my dormant paddling muscles would re-awaken at the start of the race. I was surprised to see some of my old buddies at the race. I spent some time getting used to the feel of the canoe. Soon we were all on the starting line for the 12 mile event. Not having raced against serious paddlers for a long while, I began with a moderate pace. It soon became clear that I was being left by the leaders. After an hour of paddling, a moderate pace was all I could maintain. Apparently, my paddling muscles were still in hibernation. I arrived at the finish near the back of the field in a time of two and a half hours. Racers I used to routinely beat, finished well ahead of me. In the cookout that followed the race, I was further annoyed by several people commenting on how I had "bulked up." During the long drive back to Orlando, my irritation and disappointment turned into motivation. I was going to work even harder to get back to my old shape and form.

I bought a used C-1 racing canoe, and added paddling to my fitness regimen. Monday, Wednesday and Friday mornings were gym workouts, and Tuesday and Thursday was paddling time. When I was not going to a race, I usually did a longer, slower paced canoe workout of up to three hours on the weekend. I was soon winning races again with various partners in the tandem canoe division. In 2001, Tim Dodge, a fellow paddler from Gainesville, FL, and I finished third in our division at the U.S. Canoe Association's National Marathon Championships held at Lake Lanier north of Atlanta, GA. My dormant canoe racing muscles had reawakened. I was competing at an elite level again.

During 2002, I continued to have success at canoe races around the state. I heard about a 50 mile race that was being held on the Suwannee River in North Florida. The Suwannee River flows out of the Okefenokee Swamp in Southern Georgia, and into Florida on its 220 mile journey to the Gulf of Mexico. It is one thing to take two hours to complete a ten mile race, and quite another to spend nine or ten hours doing a fifty miler. I was impressed that Marty Sullivan, my training partner in Orlando, was doing the race in a kayak. Marty is about 12 years older than me, so I figured if he could do it - I could also.

I had about two months to get ready for the Suwannee Race. When you are used to two hour races, it is quite a jump mentally and physically to do an all-day race. I immediately started increasing my weekend workouts. Two weeks before the race, I did a practice run on the Suwannee River with several other paddlers. The water level was so low that we had to drag our canoes over sand bars several times. My goal for the race was to finish the 50 miles in the daylight. At this water level, I might need some night lights to see where I am going towards the end of the race.

When race day arrived, I was pleased that the river level was up more than a foot from recent rains plus, the race director was starting us out before sunrise. That meant we would literally have all day to finish the race. All of the racers lined up on land about 100 yards from the boats, and at the sound of the whistle sprinted towards the river. It was a chaotic start, and I nearly flipped from the waves generated by the paddlers around me. As I began passing the slower boats, I was able to get into a relaxed pace. I kept my energy level up by eating snack bars and bananas every hour. My daughter, Chelsea, was waiting for me at the halfway point with another gallon of liquid. At mile 42, it was clear I would finish before dark as I carried my lightweight canoe around the class III rapid. Big Shoals is the only major rapid in Florida, and consists of two three-foot drops. After re-entering the river, I paddled down to a minor set of rapids known as the Little Shoals. I was about a half mile away from the finish, and almost through the rapids when I flipped. I muttered a few choice words, and found a shallow area to empty the water out of my canoe. I was able to re-float the canoe and make it to the finish line. My total race time was ten hours exactly, and I finished in third place overall. I now knew I was capable of paddling all day. This race had elevated me from marathon paddling to ultra-marathon paddling. I was already thinking about longer races.

CHAPTER 2

THE EVERGLADES CHALLENGE 2003

In 2003, I was ready to expand my horizons once again. I contacted a paddler from South Florida who was looking for a partner to do the 300 mile Everglades Challenge. This race starts on the shore of Ft. Desoto Park on the edge of Tampa Bay, and continues nonstop down the coast to Key Largo. The race is open to any vessel that can be launched from the beach, and does not have a motor. There are three checkpoints racers must sign into along the way. My partner, Mike Gutierrez, was about my age and would also be doing this race for the first time. He had an 18 ½ ft. Kevlar® canoe that he had modified with storage bins, a spray skirt, a sail with outriggers and a battery powered bailer. Mike had basically turned a racing canoe into a small sailboat. We met several times for training runs at the starting point in Ft. DeSoto and in the Everglades.

There is a major difference between racing all day, and racing around the clock for several days. The Everglades Challenge has no requirements pertaining to rest breaks. To do well, racers need to sleep as little as possible. I brought some caffeine gels for this problem.

The biggest issue when racing in the Gulf of Mexico or the Atlantic Ocean is one of safety. Paddlers in canoes and kayaks can be flipped over by manatees, manta rays and even sharks. Before we were allowed to race, Mike and I had to demonstrate we could get back in our capsized canoe in deep water. Of course, this was under ideal conditions. If we were in the middle of a storm with six foot waves, it would be harder and I'm not sure we could do it. Should disaster befall us, we have an E-PIRB transmitter that when activated will direct the U.S. Coast Guard to our location.

In the pre-dawn hours of Saturday, March 8th, we were busily getting our canoe loaded in anticipation of the 7 am start. There were about 40 vessels of all shapes and sizes ready to be launched from the beach. The most popular craft seemed to be kayaks and sailboats. In our class, we had the option of using a sail or paddles. We heard the sound of the air horn, and quickly pushed and pulled our heavy canoe into the surf. We jumped into our seats, adjusted our spray skirts and off we went. Mike and I had to choose between heading out into the Gulf or crossing the channel to the Intra Coastal Waterway. Mike opted for the Gulf, hoping to find some favorable winds for our sail. The winds turned out to be very light, but we made steady progress with our paddles. We arrived at Placida, the first checkpoint, at 1:39 am. Our plan is to sleep a few hours, and be on the water by dawn. Neither one of us brought an alarm clock however, and we overslept by more than an hour. That was the beginning of a bad day. Mike then made a navigation error that caused us to go to the east side of Pine Island instead of Sanibel Island. That was about a 20 mile mistake. The rest of the day we spent battling headwinds, and bailing water out of the canoe that was coming in under the canvas cover. We pulled ashore around 1 am at a park near the town of Estero. Mike and I were both exhausted, and decided to just get in our sleeping bags instead of setting up our tents. I had just gotten to sleep when I was awakened by a bright light, and the voice of an Estero policeman asking what we were doing in the park. I told him about the race, and he was very reasonable. He told us to make sure we were out of there by dawn. "No problem officer." This must be what it is like to be homeless.

The third day of the race went much better. We made good progress heading down the southwest coast past Naples. It was night time as we approached Marco Island, and a fog had settled on the water giving us an eerie feeling as we paddled forward. I spotted a red light through the fog that we were heading towards, and wondered what it could be. Suddenly a catamaran sailboat appeared in front of us. It was another Everglades Challenge competitor known as the Crazy Russian. He had hit a bridge piling earlier in the race, and had to stop regularly to bail water out of a cracked pontoon. Mike and I offered to help, but he said he was fine.

We checked in at the small village of Chokoloskee at 4 a.m., and to our surprise we were in fifth place overall. I guess a lot of racers had a bad day on Sunday. This time we put up our tents, and slept for a few hours.

We left Chokoloskee about 8 am after eating a few breakfast items from the local store. Soon we had a decent wind at our backs, and were able to stop paddling and let the wind in our sail propel us along. For three hours, I relaxed and enjoyed the beautiful scenery. We saw dolphins once in a while as we passed by the white, sandy beaches on the many islands. Florida's southern coast has over a hundred small islands bordering the Everglades. I will definitely return for a recreational camping trip. The winds started to shift as evening approached, and it was time to start paddling again.

Mike's plan was to cut through the Everglades to get to our last checkpoint in Flamingo. This route would be faster than staying in the open ocean, if we could follow the correct channels. It would have been a much easier task in the daylight. As it turned out, Mike and I spent a frustrating night wandering from one mangrove island to another looking for channel markers that were few and far between. I was starting to get aggravated at Mike for getting us into this mess. Finally about 5 am I stopped paddling, and managed to get thirty minutes of sleep in the front of the canoe. Mike said he enjoyed my "downtime" as much as I did. I have to admit I was being a jerk, but a lack of sleep will do that to you. As the sun came up we finally located the little canal leading to Flamingo, and clocked in at 8:20 am, where I managed to get another 90 minutes of sleep. Unfortunately, Mike was not able to fall asleep. We set out on the final leg of the race at 10:30 am. It is only 35 miles from Flamingo to Key Largo, but in between is Florida Bay. This can be a tricky body of water to navigate. If it is low tide, or there is a strong northeast wind, even a canoe can have problems finding enough water to paddle through. The first 25 miles went by smoothly as we neared the end of our epic journey. Our progress was slowed by a headwind that began to increase after sunset. Soon Mike and I could see the lights of Key Largo. I picked up the pace, knowing that every paddle stroke was getting us closer to the finish.

About 9 am, we ran aground. Mike and I could

see the red and green lights of the channel markers of the Intra Coastal Waterway less than a mile ahead of us. We tried pulling our canoe through the shallow area, but with every step we sank up to our knees in the silt-like mud. Mike looked at the charts, and decided we needed to back out, and go further north before heading to Key Largo. That news was like getting punched in the stomach. With considerable effort, we retraced our path out of the muck. The effort of slogging through the mud coupled with being tired from paddling had left me exhausted, and Mike was beyond that. As we tried to make our way northward through what was now a howling wind, Mike was starting to hallucinate. He had not slept any since we left Chokoloskee - almost 40 hours earlier. Mike would start laughing, and talking about seeing other people in the canoe. He also had control of the rudder, and was no longer able to keep us going in a straight line. Somehow we still managed to make progress. Although it took awhile, we were ready to head eastward towards Key Largo again. That is when I saw a rocky jetty blocking our way. Mike saw it to, but by now he was too far gone to read the charts. About 1 am we grounded out on a small mangrove island. I told Mike we were done. We had reached a point where neither one of us was sure what was real and what was a hallucination. We rearranged our gear so we could sleep in the canoe. You can sleep on a rock when you are as dead tired as we were. We awakened hours later to a sunrise over calm seas, and nothing but open water between us and the finish line in Key Largo. The rocky jetty seemed to be a creation of our sleep-deprived minds. It took us only 40 minutes to paddle to the finish. Our time was 4 days, 22 hours, 27 minutes. A lot of things went wrong during the trip- poor planning, bad navigation and tough conditions, but quitting was never an option for either one of us. Mike and I came in fifth overall out of 22 finishers of the 300 mile Everglades Challenge. I was now a veteran of a multi-day race.

It takes some time to recover from an ordeal like the Everglades Challenge. Racing in salt water is much rougher on the skin than freshwater. I had a few blisters on my hands, and some raw patches on my body where my clothes had rubbed. There is also a price to be paid for denying your brain the sleep it needs. Although, I slept for ten hours after eating a huge breakfast in Key Largo, it took a few days to regain my mental abilities. Still, I did recover quickly enough to race the following weekend on the Hillsborough River near Tampa. I raced with Carl Poulsen, my training partner in Central Florida, and we won the tandem canoe (C-2) division.

I continued my full schedule of canoe races around the state. I also took over as race director for the Suwannee River Challenge to keep the event going. I won the C-2 division with another partner, George Blakely, in that race. My daughter, Chelsea, was the timekeeper. For the year, I won eleven of thirteen canoe races. I was definitely getting back to being a top competitor in the sport I love.

Watson's Place

In 2003, Mike Gutierrez and I spent a weekend paddling around the Everglades while practicing for our upcoming race. We camped at an island called Watson's Place. I had heard the island had an interesting past...I had no idea.

In the late 1890s southwest Florida was a haven for outlaws. It is doubtful any of them could have matched the evil deeds of Ed Watson. Watson was born in South Carolina in 1855, and is rumored to have killed a black man on his father's farm at the age of nine. When he was 20 years old and living in Lake City, FL., Watson killed his cousin and fled to Arkansas. There he came in contact with the female outlaw, Belle Starr. She was murdered in 1889, and Watson was arrested for the crime. He was acquitted however, due to "circumstantial" evidence.

Watson returned to Florida in 1890, and reportedly killed a man in Arcadia. Back in Lake City, he was charged in another man's death. On trial in Jacksonville, he avoided a conviction once again.

Ed Watson arrived in the Chokoloskee Bay area in the early 1890s. He purchased a 40-acre island plantation known as Chatham Bend from the widow of a recently deceased outlaw. For over a decade, his sugar cane farm thrived. Watson sold tons of cane syrup to buyers in Ft. Myers and Tampa. He transported the syrup on his 70 ft. schooner, and sometimes returned with laborers for his farm. Watson was careful to hire mostly transients and loners. Some of the locals thought it was strange that he had such a high turn-over of workers, but Watson's reputation stopped any further inquiry.

Everything changed in 1910, when several bodies sunk with weights were found near Chatham Bend. Then a young black boy escaped the Watson farm, and told the Chokoloskee townspeople he had seen Watson kill someone. A posse was formed, and when Watson pulled up to the dock in his boat, a gun battle ensued that left the outlaw dead. Afterwards, it is estimated that over 40 skeletons were uncovered in and around Watson's Place. It seems Watson would rather kill his farm hands than pay them their wages. An inquiry was held in the death of Edgar J. Watson, but no charges were ever filed.

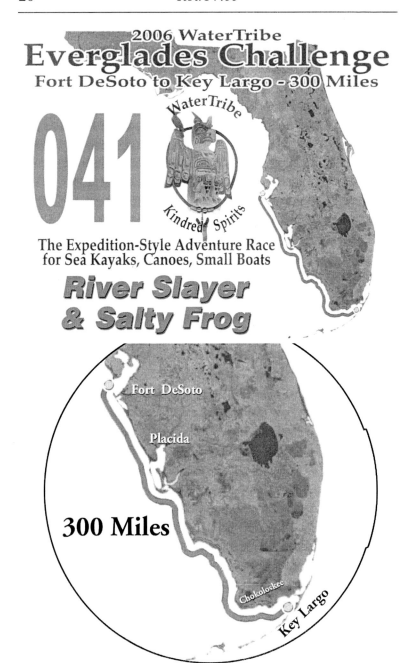

2006 WaterTribe
Everglades Challenge
Fort DeSoto to Key Largo - 300 Miles

041

WaterTribe
Kindred Spirits

The Expedition-Style Adventure Race
for Sea Kayaks, Canoes, Small Boats

River Slayer & Salty Frog

Fort DeSoto

Placida

300 Miles

Chokoloskee

Key Largo

CHAPTER 3

Everglades Challenge 2006

In 2005, the Chesapeake Light Craft Company was seeking racers to sponsor in the 2006 Watertribe Everglades Challenge. Chesapeake has a full catalog of kayak, canoe and other small boat kits for water enthusiasts. A friend, Marty Sullivan and I responded to their offer, and were one of the two teams they selected. Marty is an avid long distance kayaker and my frequent training partner in Central Florida. We were given a choice of racing in any of their vessels. Chesapeake Light Craft could send us a finished boat which we would return after the race or we could pick a kit and build a boat that would be ours to keep. Marty and I opted to construct a 21 foot, triple kayak - meaning it has three cockpits for three people. We will use the middle cockpit to access food.

When the kit arrived in early November, I was sure we were missing something. But after unpacking the boxes, it was all there. Chesapeake uses a marine-grade mahogany plywood that is only 1/4 inch thick. We set up our boat building operation in Marty's garage in Winter Park. This was his fourth kit project, which gave this greenhorn boat builder confidence we could build something that actually floats.

Chesapeake Light Craft has a computer that precuts the plywood panels for easy assembly. Marty and I epoxied three seven-foot pieces together to make the long planks that formed the hull. We next drilled hundreds of tiny holes along the edges of the planks, and tied them together with copper wire. Once we were satisfied that the hull was symmetrical, the wire ties were tightened and epoxy was poured along the seams to hold the form. The old Indian method of stitching leather together and pouring tree resin down the seams had come a long way.

Included with their detailed plans, Chesapeake sent a video about the step-by-step building process. At certain key parts in the assembly, the narrator would stress, "Now do this correctly or its a Viking funeral," and the image of a burning boat on the water would be shown. While this was very funny, it also got the message across. For three months Marty and I worked on our nautical creation. We spent a lot of hours going over the entire kayak to make 100% certain that everything was in perfect alignment. When the hull was ready, we draped a sheet of fiberglass over it and applied the resin. We usually waited at least 24 hours for the epoxy to harden. One task at a time, the triple kayak took shape. Marty and I attached the deck, and cut out holes for the three cockpits. The rudder assembly was then put into place. The final step was applying several coats of clear varnish.

Our goal for the 2006 Everglades Challenge was to finish in under three days. I remembered a movie from the 1970s called, "Three Days of the Condor." So we christened our kayak the Condor. On a Saturday morning in late January, several friends gathered on the shore of Lake Virginia in Winter Park to watch Marty and I launch our beautiful kayak. I was impressed immediately by the combination of stability and speed the craft possessed. We had a champagne toast to celebrate the launching of the Condor. Marty and I could now turn all of our attention to training for the Everglades Challenge.

Marty and I did several long runs in the Condor during February. Marty controlled the rudder from the front cockpit, which allowed me to focus on providing the power. Because of the kayak's stability, I was able to raise my seat up six inches and use a canoe paddle. With a kayak, the paddler is usually seated close to the bottom of the craft making a double-bladed paddle more efficient. By elevating my seat, I was in about the same position as my canoe. It may have looked a little odd with Marty using a kayak paddle in the front and me using a canoe paddle in the rear, but my shoulders were much happier with the arrangement.

On March 6, 2006 I was back on Ft. DeSoto Beach ready to begin another Everglades Challenge. It had been three years since Mike Guttierez and I learned how grueling the Challenge can be. While my only expectation in 2003 was to finish the race, I had far grander aspirations for this year.

There were actually three different races being contested in the Challenge. There was the 67 mile ultra-marathon, the 300-mile challenge and the inaugural 1,200 mile ultimate challenge. The ultimate challenge continues up the east coast of Florida past Jacksonville, where the racers then enter the St. Marys River on the Florida-Georgia border. They then paddle up the St. Marys for 90 miles, and then portage their boats 40 miles to the Suwannee River in Fargo, GA. From that point, it is about 220 miles down the Suwannee to the Gulf of Mexico. The worn out paddlers will then have 180 miles to race back to the finish at Ft. DeSoto. Not surprisingly, the ten racers who were doing the Ultimate Challenge were getting all of the prerace attention. It sort of made me feel like a slacker for "only" doing the 300-miler.

At 7 am, we were all charging into the water to begin our respective journeys. Marty and I were competing in the class 1 division, which allows the use of a small sail. The wind was coming from the northwest, and I was able to set the "V" shaped sail at an angle to give us an extra push. We arrived in Placida at 7:14 pm. That was over five hours faster than the time Mike and I had in 2003. Marty and I were leading our division, and were in fifth place overall. We left Placida quickly after checking-in and filling a couple of water jugs. Thirty minutes later, we stopped at a small mangrove island to heat up some water and have a freeze-dried meal.

The open water of Pine Island Sound awaited us. We put on our spray skirts that fit around the kayak cockpits to keep us dry. Marty and I were soon in two-to-three foot waves. The Condor handled the rough water easily. It took us several hours to cross the Sound. Around midnight Marty and I decided to look for a sleeping spot. Since we didn't see any parks or open areas, we picked a house that was under construction. We each grabbed our tents and sleeping bags. Marty slept in the house. I spread my tent out on the grass and crawled in without setting it up. This "stealth" method of camping is less conspicuous and saves time. Two hours later, we were back in the kayak heading towards Sanibel Island. We were slowed by headwinds for a couple of hours, but shortly after daybreak the winds shifted to our favor. I was able to deploy the sail again. Marty and I made good progress to Sanibel, and continued on to Marco Island. The hours went by quickly, and it was soon night again. We could see Marco Island in the distance, lit-up like the Emerald City in "The Wizard of Oz." There is not any development south of Marco Island, so it stands-out against the area below it.

Marty and I paddled into the Marco River at the island. An hour later, we stopped at a bridge for another stealth camping session. Everything was going well for us. The triple kayak was turning out to be a superb expedition boat, and the weather conditions were cooperating as well. Two hours later, we emerged from our dew covered tents before dawn and started paddling towards the familiar second checkpoint in Chokoloskee. Marty had picked a route that took us back out to the Gulf and by the Ten Thousand Islands area. The islands are mostly mangroves that can disorient any seasoned sailor. We then took a short-cut through the mangrove islands at Indian Key Pass. Marty had used this route in previous challenges to get to Chokoloskee Bay. Marty and I touched shore in Chokoloskee at 8:50 am. Steve Isaac, the "chief" of the Watertribe, informed us that we were in seventh place overall and still first in the class 1 group. We took some time to have a good meal in Chokoloskee - freeze dried of course. Freeze dried meals are ready to eat in minutes after adding hot water to the packet. It is a good way to have a more substantial meal after consuming a steady diet of snack bars.

Marty was feeling tired as we paddled away from Chokoloskee. I was getting concerned that we had pushed too hard, but Marty soon regained his energy. When we reached the open water south of the Everglades, a westerly wind allowed us to use the sail again. It was a welcome boost to our spirits as well as our speed.

In the Challenge it is not unusual to go a day or

more without seeing any other racers. The small sailboats generally go further off-shore than the canoes and kayaks. As the 300-mile race progresses, the contestants become increasingly spread out. On our way to Flamingo, we spotted renowned kayaker Carter Johnson and his girlfriend, Sally Mason paddling near the coast. They were in a tandem surfski with molded seats that allow them to sit on top of the kayak. It was originally equipped with an outrigger. Their kayak paddles provided the stability to keep the surfski upright. However, if Carter and Sally stopped paddling, they risked capsizing. Now that we were into the third day, they were stopping every hour for a five minute break. Marty and I would pass them doing our steady six miles per hour, and soon Carter and Sally would go zipping by us at their seven-plus miles per hour. When they took their next break, we would catch them again. Sort of a nautical "tortoise and the hare" situation.

As we neared Ponce de Leon Bay, Marty wanted to go into the Everglades to get to Flamingo. After my 2003 experience, I was understandably nervous about taking this route again. Marty was very comfortable navigating these waters from his previous Challenges. So with darkness falling, into the Everglades we went. Marty would occasionally look at his maps as we made our way from one channel to the other. By 10 pm. I was starting to get sleepy. Since Marty had the rudder controls in the front of the kayak, I was able to lower my head, close my eyes and continue paddling. I was struggling to maintain consciousness. Hallucinations were starting to appear. The shadows cast by the mangrove islands looked liked wrecked ships as we paddled by. Another time, I opened my eyes to see big fish jumping around Marty's head. I enjoyed this apparition for a few seconds, until I realized it was the glimmering water on Marty's kayak blades.

We soon found the Buttonwood Canal heading into Flamingo. Marty and I reached the third checkpoint at 12:17 am. We were both beyond exhausted from a long day of paddling with few breaks. When Marty wanted to sleep for four hours instead of two, I wasn't going to object to that. We were back on the water before dawn. Carter and Sally had left an hour before. They were competing in a different division than us, so we were not too concerned. Marty had his nautical charts ready as we started across Florida Bay. We felt well-rested and energized for the final 35-mile stretch to Key Largo. Marty led us on a precise route around the mangrove islands and through the shallow waters of the Bay. By noon, we could see buildings on Key Largo. Marty and I increased our pace, and pulled into the finish at 1:30 pm.

Although we were over our three day goal, it was still a successful challenge for team Condor. Marty and I finished in 3 days, 6 hours, 30 minutes - setting a new record time in the class 1 division. It was very satisfying to execute an efficient trip in the 2006 Challenge, after my previous frustrating adventure. Experience and equipment made the difference. Marty's navigating was almost perfect, and I was far better prepared mentally and physically for this Challenge.

Then there was our kayak, the Condor. Competing in a vessel of our own creation was special. I thank Chesapeake Light Craft for the opportunity. The Condor easily handled the rigors of the race, which made a demanding challenge more bearable for Marty and I.

ADVENTURE RACING

Many of us became aware of adventure racing in the 1990s with the highly publicized Eco Challenges. These events usually had teams of four or five racers competing in exotic locales like New Zealand, Borneo or the Fiji Islands. Teams had to navigate their way through wild terrain as they searched for checkpoints while trekking, biking or paddling. Many of the races lasted over a week, and featured whitewater and climbing sections.

A more accessible variety of adventure racing soon appeared in the States tailored to the weekend warrior like me. The events were usually between six and twelve hours long. In the fall of 2002, I entered a six-hour adventure race northeast of Orlando. Not knowing any other adventure racers, I registered as a solo competitor. My legs were in good shape from my workout sessions on the treadmill. The water section involved using a double-bladed paddle in a short kayak. Even though it was not my specialty, I still liked my chances. What did concern me was the bike leg at the end of the race. Biking was not part of my training program. And then there was the issue of navigating with a compass, something I had never done.

The race started promisingly with a paddling leg. We ran to the river, and jumped in our boats. The two and four-person teams were using canoes. I was soon able to manhandle my little barge to the front of the pack. After about three miles, I beached the kayak with several canoes close behind. I was handed a map to begin the trekking section. I had no clue how to navigate with a map and compass, and I didn't want to lose valuable time trying to figure it out. I decided to follow the two leading four-person teams. Later, I learned this is called "bird-dogging." The strategy worked well for about thirty minutes. The lead teams had taken me to three checkpoints, and we were now heading back to the river.

Five minutes later one team went in one direction, and the second team in another. I picked one team, and stuck with them. Unfortunately, ten minutes later the team I was following figured out that the other team was on the right course. This was when I decided to use my superior navigating skills. I looked at my compass, and thought I could head north and hit the river. I would be able to follow the shoreline back to the boats. I jogged northward through the woods for twenty minutes without finding the river. Figuring my chance for a decent finish in my first adventure race was now over; I decided to head for some power lines far in the distance. I could soon see a road and some mobile homes. I knocked on the door of a mobile home, and a man in overalls greeted me. As I explained that I had gotten lost in a race, I noticed one of his eyes was looking in another direction. I tried to concentrate on his "good" eye, and asked for a ride back to the race site. He seemed reluctant until I offered him ten dollars. I never thought my first adventure race would end in the front seat of a broken-down pickup truck next to a cockeyed farmer. I had a lot to learn about adventure racing, but I knew I would soon be ready to try again.

Adirondack Facts and History

The Adirondack Park in Northern New York State comprises over six million acres, and is the largest park in the contiguous United States. The park is as big as Yellowstone, Yosemite, Grand Canyon, Glacier and Great Smoky Mountains national parks combined.

Although no settlements have been found, Algonquian and Mohawk Indians used the Adirondacks for hunting. The first Europeans entered the area in the early 1600s. The French Indian War (1754-1763) pitted the British against the French on the edge of the Adirondacks. The British built Fort William Henry on the south end of Lake George in 1755. The French built Fort Carillon on the north end of the lake. The British later captured Fort Carillon and renamed it Fort Ticonderoga.

In 1837 the region was formally named the Adirondacks. Much of the area was not explored in detail until after 1870. The Adirondack Forest Preserve was created in 1885, followed by the Adirondack Park in 1892. With forces seeking to log and develop the Adirondacks, the New York State Constitution was amended in 1894 to keep the region as "wild forest lands." Because of these protections many areas of original forest in the Adirondacks are old growth today.

Serious Adirondack devotees strive to become 46ers. To become a 46er you must ascend and descend the 46 high peaks in the Adirondack Mountains. In the original surveys these peaks were all above 4,000 feet in elevation. Modern survey technology revealed that four of the peaks are below 4,000 feet, but they remain in the 46er group. Brothers Robert and George Marshall became the first 46ers when they climbed all of the peaks between 1918 and 1924.

CHAPTER 5

The Adirondack Race Series

For five years the Adirondack Canoe Classic was the most important race on my schedule. In each race there were different challenges to overcome. In the first three years, I was acquiring the experience and fitness level I needed to compete at the top. The next two years were about staying there with different partners.

In February 2004, I met a fellow paddler named Ken Streb at a canoe race in St. Petersburg. He was looking for a partner to do the three-day Adirondack Canoe Classic 90 Miler in New York. Ken explained the format of the race. There are over five miles of portages, where the paddlers have to carry their canoes in between the lakes. The first day is the toughest; covering 34 miles and featuring three long portages. The second day is a little easier, with only one long carry and covering 33 miles. The final day is a mere 23 miles, with several short portages. Ken and I exchanged phone numbers and email info, and I told him I would think about it.

The Adirondack race is one of the most popular canoe competitions in the country. I liked the timing of the event. The race is always held on the weekend following Labor Day. The weather in New York this time of year is usually mild. One month later is the Suwannee River Challenge. If you're training for two distance races, it makes it easier when they are close together. For the Suwannee River

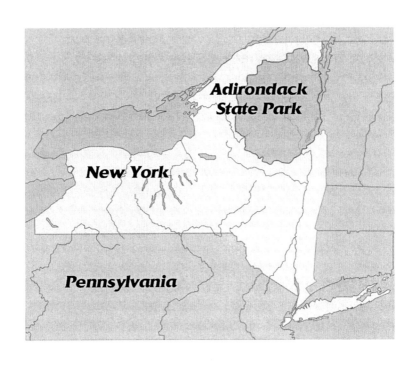

Challenge, I start lengthening my workouts in July. Doing the Adirondack race would require me to move up my schedule to June - not that big of a sacrifice. When you consider the excitement of doing a race surrounded by the Adirondack Mountains with lots of competition, it did not take a long time to tell Ken he had a partner.

Ken lives in Rochester, NY, and travels frequently with his job in telecommunications. We were able to get together for a couple of training sessions in the months preceding the race, but mostly Ken and I trained on our own. I spent many long workouts toiling in the Florida heat on the Wekiva River near my home. I also continued to do a few shorter canoe races and adventure races around the state. Before I knew it, Summer was ending and it was time to fly to New York for the Adirondack Canoe Classic.

2004 Adirondack Canoe Classic

My first Adirondack race could best be described as a humbling, learning experience. Compared to New York and the surrounding states, there are not many serious canoe racers in Florida. Because I had done well in most of my Florida events, I expected to instantly be a contender at the Adirondack race. Silly me!

When Ken and I arrived in Old Forge, New York on Friday morning to begin our preparations for the race, it was clear that I was at a "big time" event. The Adirondack Canoe Classic has a limit of 250 canoes and kayaks. Included in the canoes are C-4s (four-person canoes) and voyager canoes (six to eight people). These boats compete against each other in separate classes. Over a third of the participants enter the non-competitive touring division in any kind of craft they choose to paddle. Since they are much slower than the hardcore racers, they are allowed to start first. Then wave after wave of the various canoe and kayak classes are launched at ten-minute intervals. The shoreline around Old Forge Pond is filled with canoes and kayaks.

Paddlers are busily prepping their vessels for a day of racing. Most of them have long tubes attached to half-gallon jugs containing their favorite sports drink. Many have taped nutrition bars to the gunnels of their canoes. If you want to do well in this race, it is important to maintain your hydration and energy levels. There are not any eating or drinking breaks for serious racers. Everything is done while keeping the boat moving.

Ken and I are in the men's masters (over 40) C-2 stock division. There are 22 canoes in our group. Also starting with us are the C-2 stock open (under 40) and veterans (over 60) divisions, which add another 20 canoes. It is certainly a different feeling to be on the starting line with all these teams. There is nothing like it back home in Florida.

Race director, Brian McDonnell called our group to the starting line. He announced the names of the racers, and Ken and I gave a wave of the paddle when we hear our names. At Brian's signal the battle began, and a fury of paddles churned up the water. We lined up on the left edge of the starting line to avoid getting caught in the melee of canoes. This seemed to be a good strategy, as we heard a lot of yelling behind us from other racers trying to escape the chaos. After about an hour of paddling, we were among the top ten canoes. A lead pack of three canoes was starting to pull away. Ken and I made it to the first portage in fourth place. I was relieved to have a break from the hard pace we had been holding for close to two hours. As we made our way jogging and walking with the canoe up a long hill, we were passed by one team after another that was running up the incline with their canoes balanced on their shoulders. I estimate we had dropped to eighth place by the time we reached the next lake. This is going to be a tough weekend of paddling and portaging. I suffered through two more long carries over the next hour, and we managed to hold onto eighth place at the end of day one. Ken and I were totally spent, and we rested on the shoreline for thirty minutes watching the other racers finish. I was amazed at how far behind the leaders we were. The first place team is over 25 minutes ahead of us, and even the third place team is up by 14 minutes. Well, I did come to the Adirondacks for a challenge, and it looks like I found it. There were a lot of strong, experienced teams in this race, and beating them was not going to be easy. Ken and I had a delicious dinner back at his family's waterfront cabin, and tried to be optimistic about the next day's run.

Saturday morning we drove to Long Lake for day two's section of the 90-Miler. I was thinking that the day's pace could not possibly be as fast as day one. I was completely wrong. Ken and I were once again paddling our arms off trying to make headway in the pack. After several hours we came to the only carry of the day. The bad news is that it was a mile and a quarter long. At least it was mostly flat, and we managed to get through it without being passed. Ken and I paddled the remaining 18 miles on the Raquet River, and after posting a 4 hour 50 minute time - discovered we had moved up to fourth place in our division.

Day three passed by smoothly with a few short portages. On the last carry, we jogged past an Adirondack icon - a gray bearded, Scottish attired, bagpipe player. His music lightened my spirits and made me appreciate racing in such a scenic location. To be paddling miles along winding lakes surrounded by forested three and four thousand foot high mountains is a spectacular feeling. This makes training in the hot, humid flatlands of Florida worth it. I gave the bagpipe player a "thumbs-up" as we shuffled by. Four miles later, Ken and I sprinted for the red buoys that mark the end of our three-day competition. Our total time was 14:52:25, over 50 minutes behind the first place canoe. We both agreed - we would do better next year.

2005 Adirondack Race

Although I continued to compete in shorter canoe races and adventure races in Florida during 2005, I devoted the Summer to preparing for the Adirondack Canoe Classic. I started doing three hour workouts in June, and gradually built up to six hour sessions by the end of August. I would often go for a short jog after paddling, to get used to the sensation of trying to get my leg muscles to work after being seated in a canoe for several hours. Having experienced the intensity of last year's race, I was more focused in my training. On Monday, Wednesday and Fridays I ran three miles on the treadmill. Tuesdays and Thursdays were reserved for canoe workouts. Ken and I set a goal of finishing in the top three in our division for the 2005 Adirondack. We would have to be faster on the water, and faster on the land running with our canoe.

Once again in Old Forge, we readied ourselves for day one's competition. I recognized a few familiar faces from last year. The 2005 winners, Tim Henning and Kevin Berl were back. Third place winners Henry and Bob Donaldson from Massachusetts were also back. All of the prerace procedures were the same as last year, and we were soon battling our way to the front of the pack. An hour into the race, it was clear we were doing better than last year. Ken and I decided to try another approach to portaging the canoe. Ken had installed a carrying-yoke in the middle of the canoe. He had trained all summer running with the canoe on his shoulders. At the first portage, I quickly grabbed our paddles, life preservers and water jugs. Ken started jogging up the hill with the canoe. I was having a tough time keeping up with Ken, but our pace was much better. We completed the first carry without getting passed by our pursuers. The next two long portages went equally well. I estimated that we were in third place as we entered the Brown's Tract Marsh. This is a 2 1/2 mile winding waterway that is the last obstacle facing us on today's course. The rest of the route was all on open water. Ken and I emerged from the Marsh, and settled into a good paddling pace. With several miles to go, we spotted last year's winners, Berl and Henning, ahead of us. They were looking tired, so of course that inspired us to pick up the pace. We quickly passed them and continued charging to the red buoys marking the end of the day's section. Day one's results showed the Donaldson brothers in first place, we were in second, followed by Berl-Henning in third place. Bob and Henry Donaldson, last year's third place finishers, had over a seven minute lead on us, and it was unlikely we could catch them. Our new goal was to hold onto second place. Berl and Henning were only 32 seconds behind us. As day two started, I was hoping we could stick with the Donaldsons. Ken and I tried our hardest to get close enough to ride their wake. They were just too fast for us. We were doing well against the rest of the pack, however. Entering the Raquet River, I could not see the team of Berl-Henning. We pushed hard for the remainder of the day, and retained second place. The Donaldsons added two more minutes to their lead. Ken and I now had a 1:32 lead over the team of Charlie Bruno and Nick Hindley in third place. It was a bad day for Berl and Henning. Tim Henning was having back spasms, and they were now over 12 minutes out of third place.

The only real drama for day three was between us and Bruno-Hindley. They knew they were within striking distance of knocking us out of second place. Bruno-Hindley seemed to be full of energy for day three, and they surged off of the starting line. Ken and I were trying to keep them close, but they soon opened-up a 20 second lead. As the day progressed, they slowly increased their lead. After we completed the last half-mile portage, I estimated that Bruno-Hindley were at least a minute-thirty seconds ahead of us. We had worked hard to be in second place, and did not want to lose it in the final miles of a 90-

mile race. Ken and I rounded the bend in Saranac Lake, and saw the red finish line buoys. We went into an all-out sprint. We saw the Bruno-Hindley team cross the finish line, and continued to hammer it. Ken and I crossed the line, and slumped-over in a state of exhaustion. We had no idea how we had finished. It was not until the awards ceremony that it was announced that we held onto second place by 23 seconds. Our total time was 14:21:43. Ken and I were very pleased to receive our award plaques for being one of the top three teams in the Adirondack Canoe Classic. We had learned that increasing our training hours, and improving our portage times had elevated us into the top group of canoe racers in the 90 Miler.

2006 Adirondack Canoe Race

There was only one goal for the 2006 Adirondack Race, and that was to win it. After finishing fourth and second the previous two years, we wanted to prove we could be the best. To take the next step, Ken and I both knew we had to improve on our conditioning from the prior year. I had a very busy year of canoe and adventure racing leading up to the September race, and felt I was in great shape.

The Adirondack Canoe Classic allows six different models of canoes in our racing division. For 2006, a new model called the Susquehanna and made by Savage River Canoe was allowed. Neither Ken or I had the money available to spend close to $3,000. for the new canoe, but we needed it. We were able to rent a Susquehanna for $250. for the race. We picked up the canoe the day before the race, and spent about an hour adjusting the seats and foot braces on the lake at the Streb cabin. The canoe was definitely faster than Ken's older model.

Friday morning Ken and I drove into the small, township of Old Forge. As we readied our canoe, I noticed that our rivals from last year, team Bruno and Hindley, had also upgraded to a Susquehanna. On the starting line, the team of Kevin Ferguson and Gene Pratt were sitting in a shiny, new Susquehanna. I was now glad we had spent the money for the new canoe. It is not a good feeling to be sitting on the starting line of a canoe race knowing another team has a faster canoe than you.

At the start signal, Ken and I blasted off from the pack of 36 canoes. After one hour of racing, we held about a 20 second lead on Ferguson-Pratt. It was great to be the lead canoe in the group. This year it was our canoe that was disappearing into the horizon from most of the pack. Ferguson-Pratt gained on us in the first uphill carry, but back on the water we started building our lead again. The next two portages were the same pattern. Ferguson-Pratt could run us down on the portage, but the narrow trails would make it difficult for them to pass us. On the last long portage, they were right behind us as we walked our canoes out the boardwalk to the winding creek through Brown's Tract Marsh. It requires a lot of muscle to power your way around slower canoes and kayaks in the Marsh. Ken and I did well getting through the 2 1/2 miles, and emerged into the lake with a nice lead. We turned it on for the final 12 miles, and at the end of day one had a lead of 3:17 on Ferguson-Pratt. Bruno-Hindley were 4:35 behind us, and the Donaldson brothers were nine seconds behind them in fourth place.

The team of Price-Streb had finally made it to the top of the leader board. We had put all of our energy into the first day's run. I had really pushed myself in the portages, and was suffering through leg cramps on the drive back to the cabin. Ken was just as exhausted, and was concerned about how well we would recover for day two. We spent Friday evening resting and refueling.

Saturday morning Ken and I were both a little stiff and sore. After having my favorite pre-race meal of pancakes and doing some stretching exercises, I was feeling much better. We loaded up Ken's SUV, and drove to Long Lake for a second day of "fun" in the Adirondacks. The start was delayed thirty minutes by fog, but it was not long before our division was underway. Within twenty minutes we were leading a parade of five canoes drafting behind us. I did not want to push the pace too early. We had over a three minute lead, and I was content to keep an eye on our competition. An hour into the paddle, I spotted a C-4 (four-person canoe) coming up behind us. I steered the canoe over to the right, and the whole gang followed us. As the C-4 passed us, Ken and I doubled our pace. We jumped on the rear wake of the C-4, and began to open a gap on the boys behind us. By the time Ken and I let-up, we had a fifty-yard lead on the next canoe - which was Ferguson-Pratt. We soon left Long Lake and entered Raquet River. I noticed the river was shallower than in past years, and our progress was slowed. When we came to the 1 1/4 mile portage, I could see that Ferguson-Pratt had reduced our lead. Despite our best efforts, they caught and passed us on the portage. When we put-in on the river again, they had at least a thirty second lead. The river was still shallow and, being a lighter team, Ferguson-Pratt was pulling away from us. In the next hour, I estimated that their lead increased to about three minutes. Ken and I continued to paddle hard, but I was begining to think we were in serious trouble. Then the river started to get deeper with about six miles to go. We began to slowly creep-up on Ferguson-Pratt. Ken and I cut their lead to less than a minute, and continued to charge towards the finish line. Ferguson-Pratt must have been tired, because they did not increase their pace. At the red buoys, we finished 20 seconds behind them. Ken and I still held a 2:57 lead going into the final day. We felt like we had dodged a bullet, and I assume Ferguson-Pratt must have been depressed over letting such an opportunity get away. Once again, Ken and I needed all the rest we could get for one final day of battle.

As we lined-up for day three's competition, I felt confident we would win. The last day was all on lakes, and the portages were short. Ken and I got off to a good start, and took the lead easier than I expected. I sensed a little weakness in Ferguson-Pratt and Bruno-Hindley, who were still in third place. Over the next two hours, Ken and I put on a few sprints, and rode the wakes of faster C-4s. We opened up a comfortable lead of at least two minutes. By the time we passed the bagpipe player on the last portage, Ferguson-Pratt was not in sight. Ken and I maintained a good pace over the last four miles, and crossed the finish line in much better shape than the prior year. Our finishing time was 14:04:11. Ken and I finished 6:14 ahead of Ferguson-Pratt, more than doubling our lead. I guess we had finally worn them down. Bruno-Hindley held onto third place in front of the Donaldsons.

After three years of toil, dedication and focus, we had won the Adirondack Canoe Classic. It was very rewarding that two guys in their mid-forties could commit to a multi-year mission to win one of North America's major canoe races. The fact that the achievement took us three years, made it even more satisfying.

Adirondack Canoe Race 2007

Early in 2007, Ken Streb let me know that he was not interested in defending our title. He had wanted to win the Adirondack race for a long time, and now that he had achieved his goal, he was satisfied. Ken also mentioned how hard it was to be a repeat winner in our division. I appreciated his honesty, but I was still hungry. I liked being on top at the Adirondack, and wanted to continue my run. I had spent three years learning what it took to win the race. I was now a seasoned veteran who wanted to defend the title I had earned.

I now needed a new partner, and one paddler was at the top of my list. Roy Zweeres was 49 years old, and from Spring Hill, FL (north of Tampa). I had seen him over the years at various recreational canoe races in the Tampa area. He was usually paddling with his children, and still keeping up with the adult racers. In 2005, Roy bought a single racing canoe (C-1). I was doing a lot of C-1 races around Florida, and started seeing Mr. Zweeres on the starting line. I beat him in nine races in 2006 to win the state championship in the masters C-1 category. Roy was showing improvement with every race, however. In the first two months of 2007, I entered several adventure races in Florida. In March I drove over to Tampa for a 10 mile canoe race on the Hillsborough River. Although I was just beginning my canoe training for the year, Roy seemed to be in fine form. At the race start, he took off ahead of me. Roy steadily increased his lead throughout the race, and at the finish I was over three minutes behind him. It was a stunning reversal from the previous year. I was disappointed at losing the race, but I knew who I wanted for the Adirondack.

The following week I called Roy, and made my pitch for the New York race. I explained the format of the race, and my history of doing the event. We would need to drive to New York so we could pick up a Susquehanna from Savage River Canoe in Western Maryland. Roy said he would have to work on getting his legs in shape for the portages. I told him there was plenty of time for that, and he agreed to take on the challenge.

What marks the 2007 Adirondack race as different is what I refer to as the "saga of the back." In the 1990s, I owned and operated a paper recycling company. I frequently strained my back lifting, pushing and pulling heavy containers of paper around. I would usually take a couple of aspirin, and in a day or two was feeling okay. My company now sells office products, and moving cases of copy paper is the new threat to my back. Over the last eight years, I have had five back strains that forced me to take a few days off. The problem area is the lower spine. When it is aggravated, the normal lower back curve becomes rigid as the muscles in that area seize up. I have seen chiropractors, and sometimes their treatments helped and sometimes not. The best thing to do is just rest until the back muscles relax.

In May of 2007, I was short a delivery person for my company. A friend of mine said he would be available in September when his current job ended. I decided to do all of the deliveries until then. In the three previous years of preparing for the Adirondack, I looked at the summer months as the critical training period. In June, I would be paddling two hours on Tuesday and Thursday mornings, and on the weekends doing a three or four hour workout. By the end of August, it would be three hour sessions during the week, and six hours on the weekend. I did leg workouts at the gym on Monday. Wednesday and Friday mornings.

In the second week of June, despite trying to be careful, I strained my back delivering some cases of copy paper. It was on a Friday, and I had a long canoe workout scheduled with Roy on Saturday. I rested Friday evening, and hoped a good night's rest would help my back. It was not much better Saturday morning when I slowly rolled out of bed. I gingerly gathered my paddling gear for the workout. Loading the canoe on my SUV was very painful. I drove an hour to meet Roy on the Withalacoochee River. I did not want to alarm him, so I just said my back was a little stiff this morning. Once we started paddling, my back seemed to loosen up, and I was feeling much better. After a 3 1/2 hour workout, I said goodbye to Roy and headed home. I stopped at a restaurant, and my back had tightened up so much that I could hardly get out of my vehicle. For the rest of the weekend I did very little, and shuffled around the house like an old man.

Monday morning I called a chiropractor that another adventure racing buddy recommended. He was able to see me that afternoon. I recounted my history of back problems, and told him about my Summer workout routine that I was determined to continue. After the doctor examined my back and took a few x-rays, he said he could help me. He also advised me to take a two week break from workouts to give my back a chance to recover. That was not an option I was willing to consider. I started seeing the chiropractor twice a week, but any relief was temporary.

By July, I was in constant discomfort. I had developed a sciatic nerve problem that sent shooting pain down my left leg. Trying to sleep at night was almost comical. I had eight pillows of various sizes that I would try to arrange under my left leg and back to ease the pain. When I found the ideal position, I quickly fell asleep. An hour or two later I would awake in pain again. I was also losing weight. Chronic pain was taking away my appetite. I actually looked forward to my canoe workouts. Ten minutes into a workout the pain would subside. It would return about an hour after the session ended. I began taking a nap as soon as I returned home from paddling to get some much needed sleep. The chiropractor said I was deadening my nerves when I canoed, and it was not helping my condition. The doctor suggested I might want to try some acupuncture treatments that his associate offered. As I limped into August, I was ready to try anything. I will not try to explain the science of acupuncture, but it involves the insertion of needles at strategic points all over the body. I did not know that low amounts of electricity were sometimes run through the needles to help the process along. In one session, I had thirty needles sticking in me from my hands down to my ankles. When the attendant turned the current up too high, my left foot started flopping around like a fish out of water. I had to laugh at where my pursuit of another Adirondack title had taken me. Whether it was chiropractic or acupuncture treatments, I was still in pain.

I finally made it to September, and got some much needed help when my friend started working for me. It was time to figure out the logistics of getting to New York. My frequent training partner, Marty Sullivan, was also racing in the Adirondack. We agreed to travel together and split the costs. Tuesday morning we met at Marty's house, and started packing his SUV with luggage and gear. Marty's friend, Jack O'Connor, was going to serve as our support crew. I sat in the front passenger seat, Roy and Jack were in the back seat. We were soon on our way in one very crowded SUV. The hours slowly went by as we traveled northward. Every time we stopped for fuel, I would stretch and walk around the gas station until it was time to leave. I was taking my pain relief pills every two hours. We made it to West Virginia about 9 pm, and decided to stop at a hotel.

Saturday morning we made our way to Oakland, MD, which is less than ten miles from the West Virginia border. John Diller is the master canoe builder behind the Savage River Canoe Company. He makes some of the fastest racing canoes available in his small shop. We took about a thirty minute break to load up the Susquehanna, and to tour John's facility. This was not a mass production operation. Each canoe or kayak that John and his employee make is carefully constructed, and often customized to the needs of the buyer.

Ken Streb, my partner the last three years, had graciously invited us all to stay at the cabin. We made it to the Adirondacks in the early evening, and met Ken at the local grocery store in Old Forge to make sure our crew was well fed over the next few days. We spent the remainder of the evening relaxing at the Streb cabin after two long days of driving.

Thursday morning Roy and I took the Susquehanna out on the lake for a light workout, and to adjust the balance of the canoe. After going through my summer of agony, it was great to be back in the Adirondacks. We later went in to Old Forge to register for the race, and receive our Adirondack shirts.

Friday morning we were up early preparing our race liquids. We went over the map with Jack so he knew where to resupply us on the race route. Marty was competing in the touring kayak division. We were soon on our way to Old Forge.

Just as I was feeling it three years ago, Roy was experiencing the same excitement of being at a major canoe race. We talked over our strategy. I was confident we would dominate the other teams on the water. I told Roy that I wanted to take it easy on the portages. I believed that it would take just one slip on a rock, and my back would seize up. Of course if we were under pressure I would abandon that strategy, and do what I needed to do to win the race.

Roy and I got off to a great start. Roy paddles with a slightly wider paddle than me, and I could feel the power as we charged off the line. We were running in the lead after only five minutes. Next to us was an "open division" canoe team in the under forty class. I told Roy to get in a comfortable pace, and we will just "walk away" from everyone. The younger guy in the other canoe heard me, and had some smart remark which I did not hear. I told him that since we are in different divisions, I would be glad to run with them if they could keep up. Ten minutes later they were dropping back, and it was the Rod and Roy express pulling away from the pack.

The race was unfolding as I hoped it would. As we came ashore for the first portage, I could see the team of Bruno-Hindley about three minutes behind us. Roy and I fast walked the mostly uphill carry, and remained in the lead as we re-entered the water. My back and leg were feeling good, but there was not any need to take chances. We took it easy on the second and third long portages. Roy and I walked out on the Brown's Tract boardwalk, and saw that Bruno-Hindley were just two boats behind us. I told Roy not to worry, the rest of the day belonged to us.

Roy and I powered our way through the winding Brown's Tract run, and came out on the lake well ahead of Bruno-Hindley. It was over 90 degrees in the afternoon, which is hot for the Adirondacks. I fought through some cramps for about an hour until my electrolyte supplements took effect. Roy wanted to pull over to the shore for a quick dip in the water. I nixed that idea, and told him to splash some water on his face. I wanted to put the race out of reach on the first day. Roy finally got to jump in the water after we crossed the red buoys. An exhausted looking Bruno and Hindley team came in 7:28 behind us in second place. That was a great first day lead.

Day two went equally well. Roy and I had a big lead as we left Long Lake for the Raquette River. I was even able to shuffle along a little quicker in the only carry of the day. I had never seen the Raquet River so shallow. At times the water was only six inches deep, and we had to walk our canoe down the river until we found a deeper channel. We never saw any sign of Bruno-Hindley. Roy and I maintained a strong pace until the end of day two's run. We added another 8:31 to our advantage.

It is so nice to prepare for the last day of the Adirondack with a huge lead. Roy and I had built a 15:59 lead over Bruno-Hindley. We could have taken it easy over the last 23 miles, and followed Bruno and Hindley. Roy and I felt strong for day three, so we took it out hard again. By the end of the race our total margin of victory was 21:40. To make the day even better, Marty held off two other racers to win the men's veterans touring kayak division. When we received our plaques for winning the 25th running of the Adirondack Canoe Classic, we also were awarded a jug of beer from a local brewery to commemorate the special occasion.

Earning the victory in the 2007 Adirondack Race was especially rewarding after overcoming the physical problems I was having. I will never forget the summer of 2007, and the chronic pain that was my constant companion. I will also remember that I did not let it stop me from accomplishing my goal.

My back pain returned for the two-day drive back to Florida. I continued my canoe workouts for another month until the Suwannee River Challenge. Allen McAdams and I teamed up to win the canoe division in the 52 mile race.

At last, I was ready to take some time off. It was about two weeks later, that my back pain went away and I was able to sleep through the night. My lower spine continued to be weak, and I finally agreed to my chiropractor's recommendation to have an MRI. In February 2008, I went into a small clinic south of downtown Orlando to have my back scanned.

Without getting too technical, the results showed I had one herniated disc, two bulging discs, a bone contusion and a nerve impingement. I wondered what the MRI would have looked like last summer when I was in agony. My chiropractor referred me to an orthopedic surgeon.

A month later, I had my appointment with the surgeon. Dr. Munford was an older, experienced physician that had frequently dealt with professional athletes. After looking over my MRI scan and listening to me explain my athletic endeavors, the doctor said I could probably avoid surgery for a few years. He said I had degenerative disc disease, and to expect more back problems as I aged. The doctor advised me to be as careful as possible with my lower spine, and to call him if the pain becomes unbearable. So with that advice I decided to continue my athletic pursuits with a new motto, "protect the back." Whether I am lifting cases of copy paper or engaged in a workout, I try to avoid any direct stress on my lower back. It is my Achilles' heel, and it is not going away anytime soon.

Adirondack Canoe Race 2008

I was back in New York for a fifth straight year to take part in my favorite canoe race. Over the last few years, I had made a lot of new friends and established a few fun rivalries. This year my back problems were under control, and I was looking forward to earning another victory at the Adirondack Canoe Classic.

For the 2008 edition of the 90 Miler, I would be teaming up with Gene Pratt from Amsterdam, NY. Ken Streb and I defeated Gene and his partner in the 2006 Adirondack. In the 2007 race, Gene paddled in the C-1 stock division. I talked to Gene about possibly racing together after the '07 race, and said I would call him in Jan. Roy Zweeres decided to take 2008 off from competitive paddling, so I needed a new partner. Gene Pratt was an experienced Adirondack paddler, and he already owned a Susquehanna, one of the fastest canoe models allowed in the C-2 stock division. After the traveling ordeal I went through in 2007,it was nice to fly into Albany, and only be two hours from the mountains. Again we stayed at the Streb cabin on Seventh Lake near the race start in Old Forge. Don Pattino, a friend of Gene's, came along to serve as our support crew.

Day one of the Adirondack is the toughest of the three. The total distance is about 34 miles with about 3 1/2 miles of portaging between lakes. There were over 30 canoes on the starting line for the C-2 stock men's canoe division. The past means nothing at the beginning of the 90 miler. All teams are starting even. If you are one of the better paddlers, now is the time to prove it. Everyone is full of energy at the start, and can paddle fast. Day one is about charging off the line, and escaping the chaos of the main pack. Then you see who your real competition will be. Gene and I got off to a fair start. Having the powerful Roy Zweeres in the front of your canoe will quickly spoil you. After 15 minutes there were only two teams running with us. One was the father-son team of the Cunninghams, and the other was my constant pursuers, Nick Bruno and Charley Hindley. This year they had a brand new, carbon fiber Susquehanna canoe that was lighter than the model owned by Gene. It was clear they were ready to challenge again in 2008.

An hour into the race, we had a small lead and were able to jump on the wake of a passing C-4 canoe. The C-4 was much faster than us, but we paddled like madmen for five minutes, and tripled our margin. All of the racers were battling side-winds that caused us to paddle most of the time on the right side of the canoe. It was certainly tiring my arms out. Gene and I had about a 30 second lead when we came to the first portage at 1:40 into the race. Trying to get my legs to work is always difficult on the first carry, but we managed to hold our lead. Bruno-Hindley were not far behind us. On the next carry, which was over a mile long, they passed us. That seemed to give me a jolt of energy, and I yelled at Gene to stay with them. We had a short paddle to the Brown's Tract portage. Gene and I were in second place, and I knew the importance of not letting Bruno-Hindley open a gap on us. My legs were working better, and we actually passed them at the end of the last carry. Don and a helper efficiently switched out our drinking jugs as we entered the boardwalk leading to Brown's Tract. The boardwalk is several hundred feet long, and paddlers must walk their boats to the end without any passing. It often serves as a "timeout," as racers see where their competition is on the way to the put-in. There was not a long wait this year, and Gene and I quickly made our way into the winding river that goes through Brown's Tract marsh. Last year, Roy and I made our move at this point. It was the same situation this year, and Gene and I worked hard to get through the Tract. As we entered the lake there was no sign of Bruno-Hindley.

We were really tired from the immense energy output from paddling hard, battling rough water and gasping through three portages. But it looked like we had said goodbye to Bruno-Hindley. We entered the four mile long Marion River, and continued to hold our pace. About ten minutes into the river, I looked back and saw Bruno-Hindley closing on us. I told Gene we had company. This was practically mind blowing! We had thrown everything at these guys, and they were still coming. At one point, Gene also spotted them behind us. I continued to bear down. I was ready to "paddle to the death" before I would let Bruno-Hindley pass us on the water. We left the river, and entered another lake without Bruno-Hindley getting any closer. Gene and I entered the last lake of the day, and suddenly the Bruno-Hindley team was not in sight. We spotted those big, beautiful red buoys marking the end of day one, and sprinted to the finish. We were in first place, and much to our relief, Bruno-Hindley came in 4:47 later. From talking to Nick Bruno afterwards, it appears we both saw an illusion. He said they never got close to us after Brown's Tract. There are over 250 vessels of all kinds in the race, so maybe we saw another team that resembled Bruno-Hindley.

Day one was over, and we were exhausted. A 4:47 lead is nice, but certainly not safe in a 14 hour race. You never know how your body will recover from a six hour beating. After resting awhile, and drinking some free chocolate milk provided by a sponsor, we headed back to the Streb cabin.

The Streb cabin may have started as a cabin when it was built in the early 1900s, but it is now a full-fledged residence that can easily sleep ten people. Ken's parents, Jack and Natalie Streb, bought the property in the seventies, and have added many modern conveniences. Their children and grandchildren visit them in the warmer months, and then they head for North Carolina for the Winter. Mrs. Streb prepared a spaghetti feast for us Friday evening. Gene and I retired quickly after dinner to continue our recovery.

It is difficult to describe the feeling of being totally spent, with the knowledge that you must go through the same thing the next day. About every part of my body was sore. Gene and I carry the canoe waist-high, which bangs into our ribs and arms on the carries leaving ugly bruises. I take electrolyte supplements while I am racing, and while I am recovering. I also stay hydrated and take plenty of aspirin.

After ten hours of bed rest, we were up at 5 am for another day of war. Ken made us a filling breakfast of scrambled eggs and toast, while we prepared our powdered drinks for the race. We loaded up the SUV, and headed for the race start close to 40 miles away.

Day two of the Adirondack is thirty-three miles long with only one long portage. We paddled about an hour on Long Lake, and spent the rest of the day on the Raquette River. While the first day was warm and windy, Saturday was wet and cool. I was glad I packed my long-sleeve, poly-pro shirt. It keeps me warm even in the rain. The day two start went well, and once again we were with two other teams escaping from the pack. For about five miles Pratt-Price, Bruno-Hindley and the uncle-nephew Sennett team paddled three abreast. We had the lead, so I saw no reason to push the pace. But as we neared the Raquette River, I saw an opportunity to jump on a C-4's wake, and we opened up a gap on the other two canoes. After paddling a few more miles we came to the portage with at least a minute lead. The carry started with a hike up a rocky path. I was thinking it would be tough for Bruno-Hindley to make up any ground here. Amazingly though, shortly after reaching the top of the hill, Bruno-Hindley passed us on the portage. At least going downhill it was easier to keep them close to us. They put-in ahead of us on the river, and we quickly gave chase. The Raquette River was much deeper this year. We slowly reeled in Bruno-Hindley and passed them. Gene and I wanted to add a few more minutes to our lead. Gene had a GPS unit and was counting down the miles to the finish. At last we rounded a bend, and charged to the buoys while the crowd cheered. Bruno-Hindley came in 1:10 after us. We had hoped for a larger margin, but a 5:50 lead going the final day was substantial. Both of us were feeling lousy again. Gene went up to his SUV to recover. I found a chair and watched more racers come in while I drank about four chocolate

milks. We changed into dry clothes and drove to
Saranac Lake where Gene had reserved a hotel
room. We later went to an Italian restaurant and
re-fueled while "Uncle Don" entertained us with
stories of his many travels. Gene and I retired early
again. I was feeling a little better than the previous
night.

Day three promised to be a drier day with light
winds. It was another good start, and the same three
teams emerged again. I decided to draft behind
Bruno-Hindley and the Sennetts. We ran one canoe
behind the other as the miles counted down. The
third day has three portages. The first one is about
a half-mile long and called the Bartlett Carry. The
others are very short, involving portaging around
locks. As we approached Bartlett, Gene and I tried
to jump on a war canoe's wake. Bruno-Hindley were
ready for us, and got there first, but were unable to
stay on their wake. Gene and I stayed with Bruno-
Hindley as we portaged up the path at the Bartlett
Carry. I was so focused that I hardly noticed the
bagpipe player as we rushed by. We continued to
draft our boys after Bartlett, and I could tell they
knew this race was over. Gene and I moved ahead
of Bruno-Hindley before the last carry. Putting in
to the water with 3 1/2 miles to go, we set our
sights on finishing in less than 14 hours. Gene
and I pushed hard for the red buoys, and wound
up with a time of 13:59:06. It was the fastest overall
time in my five years of racing in the Adirondack
Classic.

Winning for the third straight time at the 90
Miler with three different partners was a special
feat. I have been fortunate to have outstanding
competitors in the front of my canoe. Not everything

goes the way you want it to in a long, multi-day event, but having teammates that never quit is mandatory for success in the Adirondack Canoe Classic.

I salute Nick Bruno and Charley Hindley for never backing down. It takes great competition to make a great race. When you have competitors that push you to your breaking point, and you persevere and emerge victorious - then you have a memorable race. Then you have a plaque on the wall that you will always appreciate.

ADIRONDACK CANOE CLASSIC
"THE 90-MILER"
Old Forge to Saranac Lake

Adirondack 90 - Masters C-2 Stock

2004	Day 1	Day 2	Total	Day 3	Finish	
Berl / Henning	6:03:35	4:35:15	10:38:50	3:22:59	14:01:49	
Greiner/McCormick	6:14:01	4:40:17	10:54:18	3:27:49	14:22:07	
H.& R. Donaldson	6:15:51	4:40:51	10:56:42	3:25:51	14:22:33	
Price / Streb	6:29:16	4:50:29	11:19:45	3:32:40	14:52:25	A long way to the top.
2005						
H.& R. Donaldson	5:47:43	4:54:24	10:42:07	3:30:56	14:13:03	
Price / Streb	5:55:05	4:56:47	10:51:52	3:29:51	14:21:43	Closer
Bruno / Hindley	5:56:08	4:57:18	10:53:26	3:28:40	14:22:06	
2006						
Price / Streb	5:42:40	4:52:54	10:35:34	3:28:37	14:04:11	1st Win!
Pratt / Ferguson	5:45:57	4:52:34	10:38:31	3:31:54	14:10:25	
Bruno / Hindley	5:47:15	4:55:51	10:43:06	3:33:19	14:16:25	
2007						
Price / Zweeres	5:41:48	5:06:08	10:47:56	3:27:47	14:15:43	1st Again
Bruno / Hindley	5:49:16	5:14:39	11:03:55	3:33:18	14:37:23	
Kosta / Stoddard	6:12:55	5:24:11	11:37:06	3:33:51	15:10:57	
2008						
Price / Pratt	5:47:48	4:47:23	10:35:11	3:23:55	13:59:06	Under 14 hrs. !
Bruno / Hindley	5:52:31	4:48:30	10:41:01	3:25:05	14:06:06	
Ross / Henning	6:01:06	4:59:46	11:00:52	3:29:21	14:30:13	

A FOURTEEN FOOT ALLIGATOR
CAUGHT NEAR ORLANDO, FLORIDA

CHAPTER 6

Gator Attack

My favorite destination in Central Florida is the Wekiva River. For a region known for its theme parks and contrived adventures, the Wekiva River presents a genuine wilderness experience. One of only two rivers in Florida that have a "wild and scenic" designation, the Wekiva has a mostly unspoiled eco-system teeming with wildlife in a sub-tropical setting. The river is located only seven miles northwest from downtown Orlando and is surrounded by 70,000 acres of state-protected lands that make up the Wekiva River Basin. The river starts at Wekiwa Springs and meanders through twists and turns for 16 miles before flowing into the much larger St. Johns River, which is 310 miles long and flows northward to Jacksonville, FL.

When I am training for a long race, I like to launch my canoe on the Wekiva at daybreak. Usually for two or three hours, I won't see another person. It is just me gliding up the river in my racing canoe surrounded by nature. My business involves driving around the city making deliveries all week. So, to be alone in a wilderness sanctuary doing what I enjoy is priceless. Even though I have been on the Wekiva hundreds of times over several decades, I am always in awe of its beauty. There are cypress and pine trees along the river, and wood storks, herons and egrets wading among the lily pads. Several times I have spotted a manatee in the shallow waters of the Wekiva.

Among the wildlife of the Wekiva River is the American alligator. For most of my paddling outings, I have been able to peacefully co-exist with the menacing looking reptiles. I would frequently see them on the shore resting. Sometimes they would ignore me, and other times they would quickly slither into the water. I never viewed them as a serious threat until a few years ago.

During 2005 and 2006, I would often meet a couple of fellow paddlers at dawn for a two-hour workout on the Wekiva River. Alligators are most active at night and into the first hours of daylight. I had a few encounters with gators during this time that got my attention.

One morning I was paddling down the river and spotted an eight-foot gator on the bank. With a big splash, it entered the river and headed towards me with its mouth open. I stopped paddling, and began hitting the water with my paddle to emulate a gun shot. Just when I thought I would have to shove my paddle down the gator's mouth, it abruptly stopped, turned around and headed back towards the river bank.

Another time, I passed a few of my training partners, and heard what sounded like a kayak hull moving though the water. My first thought was that one of my friends was sprinting to keep up with me. As I looked around to my right, there was a huge gator by the rear of my canoe keeping up with me. With an adrenaline-charged burst of energy, I was able to pull away from the gator. It soon went underwater and did not bother the other paddlers. Perhaps, it was just a curious alligator.

But it was August of 2006 that I had my closest

encounter with a Florida alligator. I was paddling
with my usual training partners, Marty and Carl.
We would meet once a week on Thursday morning
for a workout. Just to even things up, I would give
Carl a five minute headstart, and Marty a two
minute advantage. We would paddle five miles down
the Wekiva to the St. Johns River. At that point, we
would circle a channel marker and head back up
the Wekiva River. I would usually catch them shortly
after the St. Johns turn-around.

On this particular Thursday morning, I had close
to a one minute lead on Marty as I was paddling
about a mile upstream from the St. Johns. I saw
the head of a big gator in the middle of the river. I
was thinking the gator would go underwater as I
approached. When it became clear that the gator
had other ideas, I decided to go between the gator
and the shore. That left me about four feet from
the reptile. As I started to go by, I noticed it turning
to face me. I had just nervously uttered, "Hey
buddy..." when the gator lunged at me. Its mouth
was wide open, exposing a full set of sharp teeth. It
struck my carbon fiber canoe about three feet up
from the middle of the canoe where I was seated.
The attack happened in a split-second, and I was
lucky to keep the canoe upright. I was paddling
furiously with my heart about to explode. When it
was clear the gator was not chasing me, I stopped
and saw that it had gone back to its previous
position. I was wondering if it would attack Marty,
but thought I should probably warn him of the
gator's presence. As Marty neared the gator, I yelled
to him that the beast had just attacked me. He
decided to wait for Carl to catch up to him. Together,
Marty and Carl slowly approached the gator while

hitting their paddles on the water. Finally, with a big splash, the gator went underwater and they were able to pass. I looked over my canoe and discovered that one of the gator's teeth had pierced my canoe above the water line. After explaining to Marty and Carl what had happened, and regaining my composure, we resumed the workout. It was then that I noticed water coming into my canoe. Fortunately, I had a manual bailer that allowed the water to drain out, and was able to finish the workout without any more problems. I pulled my canoe from the water, and only then realized the full extent of the damage. Two of the gator's teeth had actually bitten through the bottom of the canoe, in addition to the puncture above the water line. There were also cracks on the side of the canoe from the force of the gator's bite. Judging by the size of the gator's head, we estimated it was ten to eleven feet long.

After speaking with a park ranger, I learned that the gator was most likely a female guarding her egg-mound. The ranger further explained alligator behavior to me. He said an unyielding gator is saying that you are entering its territory. If the gator has inflated its body so that you can see all of it on the surface of the water, that is a highly aggressive gator - and it is time to turn around.

I was able to repair my canoe with epoxy and more importantly, learned a good lesson in alligator behavior. I have avoided having any other serious meetings since that August incident by using basic common sense. Whether it is a workout or a race, I now stop for assertive alligators. The Wekiva River Basin is the natural habitat for the alligator. Since that day, I always remember that I am a guest in their home.

American Alligator Facts

The American alligator's habitat extends from North Carolina to the Rio Grande in Texas. In Florida, the alligator population is estimated at between one and two million. They are found in rivers, swamps, marshes and lakes. Alligators do not have salt glands, and can only tolerate salt water for brief intervals.

The average size for an adult male alligator is over 11 feet. Large males can exceed 14 feet, and weigh more than 1,200 lbs. Female adults are several feet shorter in length than the males. The armored skin on the back of alligators is composed of bony plates called scutes. They have five toes on their front legs, and four toes on their hind legs. Alligators have long snouts with upward facing nostrils, that allow them to breathe while the rest of their body is underwater. Alligators reach adulthood between 10 and 12 years, when they are approximately six feet long.

Female gators build nests up to ten feet in diameter and three feet high. In late June or early July, the female lays around 50 eggs, and covers them with vegetation. After a two-month incubation period, the baby gators are ready to hatch. The sex of the juveniles is determined by the temperature in the nest. Over 93 degrees F. will produce all males, and below 86 degrees F. results in all female. Temps. in between will produce both sexes. Young alligators grow about one foot each year. Female gators protect their young for several years, until they leave to establish their own territories. The life span for wild alligators is about 50 years.

From 1973 to 2006, there have been 17 human deaths attributed to alligators in Florida. In one week in 2006, three people were killed by the reptiles. As the alligator population continues to increase, and their habitat decreases from development, there are likely to be more gator-human encounters in the future.

Circle represents the area of the Raft Race near the headwaters of the Amazon River. The highlighted area shows the entire Amazon River Basin. Water from 40% of the South American continent drains from the basin into the Great Amazon River.

CHAPTER 7

The Great Amazon River Raft Race

To be a true adventure racer, an athlete cannot limit themselves to one type of event. A race does not have to have a canoe in it to be attractive to me. Traveling to a foreign country and experiencing another culture is adventurous in itself without any competition being involved.

In April of 2008, I was contacted by Anita Allen, a marathon runner and kayaker from South Florida, about doing a raft race on the Amazon River in Peru. I met Anita at the Suwannee River Challenge a few years ago. She was a good kayak racer, and a tough competitor. Anita said she was trying to put together a four-person team for the race in September. She gave me the website on the race to learn more about it.

The Great Amazon River Raft Race is billed as the world's longest at 132 miles. It is a three-day stage race, with each stage being about 40 miles long. Racer must construct their own rafts out of pre-cut balsa logs the day before the event. The race starts in Nauta, Peru and ends in Iquitos, Peru.

I was a little concerned about the timing of the competition. The raft race was less than two weeks after the Adirondack Canoe Classic. To turn my attention to another major event in such a short time frame wouldn't help matters. Racing in Peru would probably cost at least $2,000. for a week including airfare. When I thought about the pros and cons of doing the race, it came down to this - How often do you get the opportunity to be in a raft race on the Amazon River? I might never have the chance again. And as for the expenses, I always say, "Never let money stand in the way of adventure."

The next day I emailed Anita to let her know that she had another team member. She also had a commitment from Greg Talik, a paddler that lived near her in the Ft. Lauderdale area. That meant we had just one more seat left to fill on the raft. I contacted several of my adventurous friends, and one of them, Dave Knothe, jumped at the chance. Dave's specialty is biking, but he is also a decent kayaker. For this race down the Amazon, Dave would be using a canoe paddle. And because he lived near my house, I would personally help with his transition from the kayak paddle to the canoe paddle. It would be nice to have some company on my long weekend workouts.

Since it was Anita's idea to do the raft race, she was the defacto captain of the team. We registered for the race as the "Florida Four," and sent our $400. to Peru. Because this would be the first time in Peru for all of us, we decided to arrive on the weekend before the race to do some sight-seeing. Anita did a good job of taking care of the logistics. From flight info. to lodging, she kept us informed with a steady stream of emails. We had several choices for accommodations during the raft race. Option "A" involved staying in air conditioned comfort aboard the plush Dawn on the Amazon Yacht. Option "B" was an un-air conditioned riverboat where we would sleep in hammocks. Option "C" meant going to shore at each village to sleep on the floor in a communal area established for the raft racers. Option "A" was very high dollar, and wasn't the idea to have a jungle experience. Assuming the Peruvian climate could be no tougher than Florida, we decided to skip the air conditioning. Option "C" was the cheapest choice, but a little too confined for our taste. So it would be hammocks on the riverboat. The next item we needed to be concerned about was the construction of the raft. According to the rules, teams would select at least eight five-meter long balsa logs to build the raft. You were allowed to alter the first and last meter of each log, which usually meant shaving each end into a point for better movement through the water. When I looked at the website it seemed that most teams built their rafts by just lining up eight logs together. This required racers to paddle on one side for long periods. Teammates would have to switch places to the other side of the raft to avoid tiring their arms out. I thought of building a pontoon style raft to alleviate this problem. We would have at least four logs on each side with about a two foot gap in the middle. Three wooden cross pieces would hold the craft together.

Because we would not have to change positions, we could arrange our seats to make sure the raft was running level in the water. I also noticed from the website photos that most racers were sitting on the logs as they paddled. In addition to having a poor paddling posture, this increased their exposure to parasites in the Amazon River. I planned to build a six-inch high, lightweight pedestal with a canoe seat that could attach to the raft. My teammates agreed, and I ordered four seats from a canoe manufacturer. Dave bought a few hundred feet of rope to hold all of the logs together.

He showed us how to tie the most efficient knots, which we practiced during the months leading up to the race.

While it would be preferable to actually paddle a raft while training, it was not feasible. Instead, we met several times to workout in heavy-duty recreational canoes. Dave and I had a few long training sessions on the Wekiva and St. Johns Rivers.

In the week before leaving for Peru, I prepared a list of everything I might need. The only thing I planned to buy for the race was bottled water. Even though it was not the rainy season in the Amazon, I made sure I packed clothing that would keep me comfortable in wet weather.

I met Dave at noon on Friday at his home in Orlando, and we drove down to Anita's house in Ft. Lauderdale. Greg arrived an hour later, and we transferred our gear into one SUV. It took me about ten minutes to make a cardboard box to hold our carbon fiber racing paddles. We then went to a local restaurant for our last meal on North American soil for awhile. After dinner, we had a thirty minute drive to Miami International Airport. Our flight was not departing until 1 am, and was nonstop to Lima, Peru. All of us cleared the security and customs checks without a problem. I was starting to doze off when we were finally called to board the LAN Airways plane. The flight crew seemed as competent as any on a U.S. carrier I had flown with. So with the confidence that we had a better than average chance of reaching our destination, I quickly fell asleep after take-off. We landed in Lima around 7 am. Anita had scheduled our flight to Iquitos at 5 pm to allow us time to see the capital of Peru.

Lima was founded by Spanish conquistador Francisco Pizarro in 1535 after defeating the Incan ruler Atahualpa. The city is dominated by a 500 ft. high Andean foothill named San Cristobal. Pizarro placed a large, wooden cross on top of the hill which can still be seen today. Lima became a regional center for trade, and saw continual growth over the next four centuries. Despite devastating earthquakes in 1687, 1746 and 1940, the inhabitants always rebuilt their city.

In 2006, Lima's metropolitan population was estimated at 8.4 million people, making it the 18th most populous city in the world. The population density is three thousand people per square kilometer, which is very crowded.

Leaving the Lima airport for a tour of the city, the first thing that caught my eye was a sprawling shanty town that must contain thousands of Lima's poorest residents. I then noticed that many of the buildings appear to be functional, but not completely finished. Our guide tells us that this is intentional. When a building's construction is finished it is assessed for taxes. The landlords are taking advantage of a loophole in the Lima tax laws.

Our first stop is the San Francisco Monastery. Construction of the church was completed in 1774. The monastery has an impressive collection of religious artwork and paintings. It served as Lima's first cemetery, and thousands of bodies were buried in the catacombs beneath the church. We walked through the narrow hallways, and I was surprised to see bones and skulls arranged in decorative patterns like artwork. At some point, the monks took apart skeletons bone by bone to create this morbid attraction. That must have been an interesting job.

We had lunch at a modern shopping development built on a cliff overlooking the Pacific Ocean. From our restaurant we had a great view of the shoreline. We all shared a seafood appetizer, and later strolled through the shops. I noticed a policeman at the entrance to the complex keeping a few poor beggars from entering.

The final stop was the Plaza de Armas. This is the historic center of Lima, which includes the Governmental Palace, the Cathedral of Lima, the Archbishop's Palace and the Municipal Palace. There is a heavy police presence here, and our guide told us that until a few years ago this area was not safe for tourists. After a busy afternoon in Lima, which gave me a better understanding of the Peruvian culture, we returned to the airport. The window seat I had on the flight to Iquitos gave me a spectacular view of the Andes mountains. Once we were past the mountains, there seemed to be endless jungle. I didn't see any signs of human development until we neared Iquitos, Peru.

After landing and exiting the plane onto the tarmac, I received my first surprise. I was not engulfed in a swarm of giant mosquitoes and other biting insects of the Amazonian jungle. I had expected to see at least a few of the blood-suckers buzzing around, but I had more mosquitoes in my back yard than here in Iquitos. We had all received yellow fever and hepatitis shots along with malarone pills for malaria before leaving the States. Our hotel had a mini-bus waiting for us, and we loaded our luggage and gear on board, and left for downtown Iquitos. We quickly learned we were in the city of the moto-kar. These are small motorcycles attached to a two-wheel rear axle. Iquitos has over 40,000 of the noisy, little machines. It seems like most of the moto-kars are used as cabs. Money is scarce, and there are plenty of men hustling for a few dollars. There is quite a competition among moto-cabs to shuttle tourists around the city.

Following check-in at the hotel, we decided to walk down to the Amazon riverfront. We saw another U.S. team at a little restaurant, and joined them. It was the all-star "Easy Living" team that would have to be the pre-race favorites. I recognized Carter Johnson from when I raced against him in the 2006 Everglades Challenge. The team captain was David Kelley, an elite adventure racer from California. I had also heard of West Hansen from Texas. They were still waiting for their fourth teammate to arrive from Hawaii. We drank a couple of beers and consumed a few slices of pizza, as we talked about the raft race without divulging any confidential race strategy. We were seated in front of the restaurant, and were frequently interrupted by passing street vendors selling native bracelets, necklaces and other trinkets. It was easier to just ignore them, and avoid making eye contact as we continued our conversation.

The fun evening came to an abrupt halt, when Anita realized that her purse was gone. It did not take a Sherlock Holmes to figure out that the likely suspect was one of the street vendors. Unfortunately, Anita's purse contained $600., her credit cards and her passport. After an initial search of the area, Anita walked to the nearest police station to report the crime.

Back at the hotel, we reassured Anita that everything would be okay. She planned to contact the U.S. embassy the next day to see about obtaining a replacement passport. Anita had already cancelled her credit cards. We gave her some cash, until her son could wire her some money. Anita's unpleasant experience reminded the rest of us to be more vigilant. While we might be prepared for the dangers of the wilderness, it is the criminals in the city we have to watch out for.

Sunday morning we boarded a long, narrow motor launch for a short trip up the Nanay River to visit the Bora tribe. According to our guide, the Borans had settled in this area 45 years ago after fleeing their native Columbia where they were being hunted by another tribe. We are led to a large pavillion-like structure of native construction. The chieftain bangs a large tribal drum, and Borans start emerging from the jungle. We learn that they make all of their clothes from plants found in the area. They demonstrate some of their tribal dances, and Anita and I are volunteered to dance with them. If you are going to look foolish, it is best to do it in another country. The grand finale of the program is when the tourists are separated from their cash. The Borans bring out lots of handcrafted jungle jewelry and other tribal items. Dave bought a monkey skull necklace, which I thought would likely be seized by Customs agents. I bought a sloth claw necklace, and a miniature blow gun. Our questions about why a jungle tribe needed money were answered a few days later, when we spotted the Borans headed for Iquitos in regular street clothes. Another innocent tribe is corrupted by the lure of the big city.

We returned to Iquitos for lunch, and then met the defending Amazon raft racing champs, Los

Increibles. As their name would suggest, they had dominated the raft race for years. These guys were all shorter than us, and each of them probably weighed less than 120 lbs. Our initial goal was to get some tips on their raft building techniques, but we decided instead to hire them and their machetes to assist us. They even let us try out their practice raft on the river. The Incredibles did not seem too concerned about the Florida Four beating them.

Later in the afternoon, we checked out of our hotel, and boarded another motor launch for a 50 mile trip up river to the Heliconia Amazon River Lodge. Anita had arranged a two-night stay in this remote setting to give us a real Amazonian jungle experience. This was the "low water" time of year, and when we arrived at the lodge we had about 50 feet of shaky steps to climb up the muddy bank. We were met by the official lodge greeter, and a guy holding a cute baby sloth. He gave the sloth to me, and it instantly latched onto my shirt with its long claws. The baby sloth then crawled up to my head and became entangled in my hair before the jungle guy retrieved it. I was wondering if I now had Amazon sloth fleas.

Considering it is surrounded by jungle, the Heliconia Lodge is very impressive. The entire complex is built on wooden stilts, and features 20 guest rooms, a bar and lounge along with a spacious dining hall all built in rustic, native-style construction. The lodge has its own water treatment system. Power is supplied by an electric generator that is used for two hours in the morning and five hours in the evening.

We had a great time at the lodge. Our young guide took us on a long hike through the jungle.

He showed us the Remo Caspi tree, which literally means "paddle tree." This is the tree that the locals carve their spade-shaped paddles from. We went fishing for piranhas in the Amazon River. I think we all managed to catch at least one. Our guide took us upriver a few miles, and we were able to catch glimpses of the rare, pink Amazon river dolphins.

The food at the lodge was excellent. We enjoyed a healthy diet of potatoes, river rice, papaya, melon, chicken and several types of Amazon fish. As much as I enjoyed the food, I think this is when the local bacteria started causing havoc with my intestinal tract.

I started feeling poorly Tuesday morning as we prepared to leave, and by the time we made it back to our hotel in Iquitos, "Atahualpa's Revenge" had taken hold. I spent the rest of the day in bed, when I was not dashing to the bathroom. I was alternating between being feverish to having the chills. My teammates checked on me throughout the day. I was concerned that my illness might not end before the raft race. Although I did not have an appetite, I ate some snack bars I had brought for the race. I was too sick to attend the raft racers reception in the evening. With my energy level at zero, I stayed in bed and slept sporadically through the night.

Wednesday morning I was feeling slightly better. Today we were going to take a river boat up the Amazon to the town of Nauta, where the raft race would start. I slowly packed my luggage, and joined the gang in the hotel's dining area. I was not interested in eating anything. After breakfast, we squeezed into some moto-cabs with all of our gear and luggage, and rode down to the waterfront.

Awaiting us at the dock, was the Miron II, a classic Amazonian riverboat. We boarded the two-level vessel, and staked out an area on the first deck. The second level was already full of raft racers. We hung up the hammocks that we had purchased in Iquitos. I grabbed four plastic chairs to complete our little enclave. I then settled into my hammock to continue my recovery.

The Miron II was definitely not a speed boat. We were going against the strong current of the Amazon River. Also, with 50 racers and their gear crammed into a space designed for 25, the boat was probably overloaded. As the Miron II chugged upriver, dinner was served by two attractive young senoritas. I handed my plate to Greg. I was not going to take any more chances with the local cuisine. It was soon night time, and everyone started making preparations for sleep. We had a loud group next to us from San Francisco, CA, that I dubbed the "gay alliance" for obvious reasons. We arrived in Nauta about 1 am, and several members of the alliance thought that was cause to celebrate. After waking up the whole boat, some guy said what I was thinking, and yelled, "Shut the hell up! We are trying to sleep." That seemed to get the message across, and the rest of the night was uneventful.

Thursday morning we gathered with the other racers in Nauta's plaza de armas for a civic reception. After listening to the town's not-ready-for-primetime, eight-member band stumble through a few songs, we were officially welcomed to Nauta by the mayor. Miniature key-chain paddles were handed out to the rafters to commemorate the event. Nauta has the distinction of being the first city on the Amazon River. In 2005, a 100 mile road to Iquitos was completed, which reduced travel time from 12 hours by riverboat to 1 1/2 hours by bus. The third-world town currently has a population of 11,000, but it is starting to grow with its easy access to Iquitos.

At 1 pm the rafters were ferried across the Amazon to the Isla de Pescadores - Fisherman's Island. Dave grabbed his gear bag, and we set up in an area on the shore to build our raft. There was a big pile of precut balsa logs. Teams were called in the order that they had registered for the race. The Florida Four was number 12, and we were able to pick some decent logs. There were a total of 46 teams entered. The last five or six teams had some bent and twisted logs to choose from.

We arranged our logs in groups of four. The Los Incredibles joined us with their machetes, and quickly went to work shaving the ends of the logs into points. Dave had bought three wooden, cross pieces at a lumberyard in Iquitos, and we nailed them on top of the logs in the front, middle and back of the log pontoons. We were about to tie the logs together with our rope when one the Incredibles showed us the much thinner twine that they use. They proceeded to quickly tie the logs together using a technique they had perfected from their years of raft racing. They then left to make some more money helping other teams with their rafts.

Our next task was to attach our seats to the raft. Since I was the heaviest, I put Anita in front of me, and Greg and Dave on the other raft pontoon. I was able to raise my seat about six inches with some plastic foam I had brought from Florida. When we were all satisfied with the finished product, we took the raft out for a practice cruise. I was in charge of steering, and I was pleased at how well our craft was handling. The raft maintained its rigid shape, and we were able to paddle on both sides of the pontoons. Our raft sat low in the Amazon, and the river water flowed through the raft as we paddled. After a successful outing, we pulled the heavy raft back onto shore to await tomorrow's race.

Thanks to the Incredibles, we were among the first teams to finish our raft. We decided to walk around the island to watch the other crew working on their logs. The most common design was eight logs across. I was confident our raft would be superior to these. But when I saw what the Easy Living team was building, I was further impressed. They were making a ten meter long raft by fastening one group of four logs in front of the other. They were fortunate to be the third team to pick their logs. Their design was made more efficient by having straight, equally sized logs. They used long bolts and steel cables to hold the craft together. Easy Living then coated the entire raft with blue paint to waterproof the logs. They were certainly prepared.

Although I was still feeling weak, my intestinal problems had stabilized. I was eating more protein bars and some of the small, Amazonian bananas. It was now Dave's turn to be sick. He was having the same symptoms I was, and had slept very little the night before. Dave had brought a sleeping bag with him, and decided to sleep on the island instead of the crowded riverboat.

I awoke from a restful sleep on Friday morning, and immediately went into my pre-race routine. We expected today's stage to take between five and six hours. I mixed up 1 1/2 gallons of my favorite protein and electrolyte high-endurance drink. It would have been nice to have one more day to regain my energy, but it was now race time and my teammates were counting on me. We arrived at Fisherman's Island at 7 am, and began loading our drinks and food on the raft. Poor Dave had another bad night. He said some of the British racers camped on the island and partied until 3 am.

It was an amazing sight to see all of the 46 balsa wood rafts along the shoreline. There were 12 Peruvian teams and 34 international teams. A total of 15 different countries, as far away as New Zealand and Australia, were represented in the race. A goofy-looking guy walked over to me, and said he was a journalist from Ireland. He asked me a few questions about the race. When he wanted to know who was favored to win, I truthfully told him that the Easy Living team would be hard to beat. He then enlightened me with some of his brilliant raft racing strategy. He said, "If I was you, I would paddle as hard as you can to that first bend in the river. If you can get ahead of them at the start, you might just break their hearts." And there you have it - the "break their hearts" strategy of raft racing. I wondered what kind of mind altering substances my Irish friend had been taking.

The race was scheduled to start at 8 am. It would be impossible to have the rafts line up across the Amazon River. The current was too strong. A few minutes after 8 am, I watched the raft race organizer, Mike Collis, make his way to the shoreline. I knew what was coming, and told the crew to take off. We had a clean start, while many of the rafts were bumping into each other as they left the river bank. Collis was waving a towel and shouting, "Go, go..go!" The tenth running of the

Great Amazon River Raft Race was underway. Five minutes into the race, I could see that the blue raft of the Easy Living team was in the lead followed by a team of Peruvians. We were in third place, closely followed by two other Peruvian teams. Several minutes later I noticed an official looking motor launch passing all of the rafts and heading downriver. As it went by the lead blue raft, it pulled in front of them- stopping their progress. At first I thought the Easy Living team was in trouble, but then I saw the Peruvians on the boat waving their hands and yelling "alto" to all of the rafts. They were stopping the race. Of course we were wondering what was going on, as all of the rafts bunched up behind us. I could see that the Easy Living crew was very angry. Then a Peruvian in a suit stood up in the boat. He raised his arm and blew a whistle, and the race was restarted. We learned afterwards, that the local district politico on the boat was supposed to be the designated race starter. He was obviously upset when he arrived after 8 am to see that Collis had given the "go" signal. I am curious about who had the bright idea of stopping the raft race so he could restart it. Welcome to third-world South America!

Once underway again, we slowly emerged from the pack. The blue raft was leading again, followed by Los Incredibles. I guess all of that pre-race machete work had not tired their arms out. There were two more Peruvian rafts in front of us, and another right behind us. Our group of six rafts was opening up a wide gap on the rest of the rafting group.

There was quite a contrast between the typical Peruvian team and ours. We had light-weight, carbon fiber paddles. They had heavy, wooden paddles. We wore expensive sports attire from our hats, to our perspiration-wicking clothing, to our fancy sandals. They wore their normal street clothes. Some of them had made wide-brimmed hats from palm fronds. We had drinking tubes connected to gallon jugs containing advanced endurance drinks. Those that did not drink straight from the Amazon, had a few plastic water bottles. We had an assortment of protein and energy bars. The Peruvians brought along a bunch of bananas. And yet, we were getting our butts kicked by three of the teams, and struggling to stay in front of another.

I was paddling very hard the first two hours, and then I seemed to run out of energy. We were passed by the fourth Peruvian team. By the third hour I was exhausted. I turned over the steering duties to Greg in the front of the raft. Even though I was eating and drinking, I was still weakened from dysentery. Dave had been struggling for several hours, and had even vomited a couple of times. We were both feeling dizzy and shaky. I didn't know if I could make it another two or three hours. Thankfully, as we approached the four hour mark and rounded a bend in the river, I could see our riverboat anchored on the shore at a village. We saw the raft in front of us paddle towards the village. It was the finish of the first stage. We arrived at the small village of Porvenir in sixth place. Dave and I had survived to paddle another day.

We pulled our raft up the riverbank, and I stumbled back onto the Miron II. I was ready for some serious recovery time. Unfortunately, this was not the Adirondacks. There was not a cold drink and an air conditioned room waiting for me. This was the Amazon jungle, and as I settled into my hammock, I was still sweating.

I decided to take a shower before the rest of the rafters arrived. The bathroom facilities on board our riverboat were very basic. To flush the toilet, you dipped a one-gallon bucket into a 50-gallon barrel that was outside the wooden stall, and dumped the water into the commode to flush it. Your waste then went straight into the Amazon River. A shower nozzle was located over the toilet. Every morning the deck hands filled up eight 50-gallon barrels on top of the riverboat's second level with water from the Amazon. This is the water we showered in. I was careful when rinsing off to keep my head down and my mouth closed.

After we had all "freshened up," I joined my teammates for a walk around the village. Porvenir was much smaller than our launching point of Nauta. There appeared to be only one convenience store / saloon. The village's lone industry was a small rum distillery. We watched as a worker fed sugar cane into a mechanical press to begin the rum making process. Some of the rafters bought bottles of rum. The Florida Four decided to stay sober on Friday night. It was almost midnight when the Amazonian heat seemed to relent, and I was able to sleep comfortably.

Saturday morning the racers were busy getting their rafts ready for another fun day on the Amazon. We learned that the Easy Living team had a seven minute lead on Los Increibles. It was the first time a foreign team had ever been in the first position. I think we were about ten minutes behind the fifth place raft. They must have been worried, because they had rebuilt their raft into a pontoon design like ours.

The start of the second stage was more chaotic than the first day. The shoreline was so crowded that some of the teams had to wait to launch their rafts into the river. We were briefly blocked by two rafts, but were soon churning forward. After fifteen minutes, the same six rafts were pulling away from the main group.

It was difficult to judge where the fastest current was on the wide Amazon River. If anyone knew, it would be the Peruvian teams. So our strategy was to follow them. Anita had a GPS unit on the raft, and it measured our speed at between three and seven miles per hour for most of the race.

Saturday turned out to be a scorchingly hot day. There was very little cloud cover, and I remembered that our location was just a few degrees below the equator. The heat was as intense as anything we experienced in Florida. We eventually took turns splashing each other with our paddles to cool off. I tried not to think about how polluted the river water was that we were dousing ourselves with.

The raft racing teams were told to look for a narrow channel on the left side of the river. It was a shortcut, and would save us several miles. We found the channel after about three hours of paddling. The current increased as we entered the inlet, and I steered away from some submerged trees in the water. We learned later that a Canadian team busted up their raft when they hit the trees, and had to be rescued by a support boat. There were lots of plants and trees floating down the river. We were constantly hearing splashes, as large chunks of dirt fell into the river. I would not want to own riverfront property here. As one local Peruvian said, islands appear one day and disappear the next on the Amazon River.

Dave and I were both feeling better that second day despite the heat. We were all eating bananas that were given to us in Porvenir, and the potassium was helping our energy levels. The Florida Four briefly passed the fifth place Peruvian team in the channel. It looked like one of them was not feeling well. They soon regained their focus, and began to pull away.

A cell-phone tower marked the end of the second stage in the town of Tamshiyacu. As we approached five hours on the river, I was looking for that tower around every bend. I turned over steering to Greg again. My energy was starting to wane, but I was in much better shape than yesterday. At last we spotted the tower, and twenty minutes later our tired crew landed in Tamshiyacu, Peru.

Tamshiyacu has a population of around 3,000. It is an agricultural community that supplies pineapple, umari, cashews and Brazil nuts to Iquitos. Since it had a cell-phone tower, I was hoping it might have an ice cream shop. I desperately wanted something cold in my system. As soon as Dave and I cleaned up, we set off to explore the town.

We didn't find an ice cream shop, but we did get some cold drinks at a cafe. Later, we ran into the Easy Living team at a tavern, and joined them for a reasonably cold beer. They had added to their lead with another stage win. The Los Increibles team made it interesting when they passed the blue crew midway through the run, when Easy Living picked the slower side of the Amazon to paddle on. They soon recovered, caught and passed the Peruvians. Easy Living now had a twenty minute lead on the second place raft.

There were several small hotels in Tamshiyacu, and Dave wanted to get a room. He was still not sleeping well on the riverboat. If any of the hotels were air conditioned or even had ceiling fans, I probably would have joined him. He rented a room at one of the more modern inns. The cinder-block structure was freshly painted, and had a communal bathroom with showers. Dave said he would meet us at the raft in the morning, and I walked back to the Miron II. Several hours later, as we were preparing for our last night on the riverboat, here comes Dave with his sleeping bag. It seems the toilets were overflowing with waste, and there was not any water coming out of the shower at his hotel. Dave always did have high standards.

Sunday morning the race officials reported that the fifth place Peruvian team had withdrawn from the race. That meant we were now in fifth place. The rescued Canadian team was allowed to finish the race on the Peruvians' raft.

The last stage of the race looked like it would be the shortest, at about 20 miles. We were happy that today's weather was supposed to stay cloudy and overcast. As we awaited the start, I noticed that the fourth place Peruvian raft had a female member. I was thinking we were the first co-ed team in the race, but obviously that was not the case.

We had another mass start, and easily escaped from the main pack of rafts. I estimated we were at least thirty minutes behind the fourth place raft in elapsed race time, and probably over an hour ahead of the sixth place raft. Unless something drastic happened, we were going to finish in the fifth position. We settled into a steady pace, and enjoyed our last day on the Amazon River. Two hours later we started seeing buildings on the outskirts of Iquitos.

The race ended at the Iquitos municipal pavilion on the Nanay River. It was a tough final stretch. For about 200 yards, we had to paddle our hardest against the current of the Nanay. At last we crossed the finish line to the cheers of the big crowd gathered on the shoreline. We then relaxed at a table under the pavilion, and I drank three bottles of cold soda. It was good to be back in the relative civilization of Iquitos.

The awards ceremony was disappointing for the Florida Four. In spite of being the second foreign team, the second co-ed team and the fifth overall raft, we received nothing. Cash prizes and plaques were awarded to the top three teams, and the winners of each division. The Florida Four had the second best finish for a foreign team in the history of the raft race. We just had the misfortune of competing in the same year as the Easy Living squad. Easy Living not only won, but set a record for having the fastest time. It should also be noted, that they donated their prize money to the other Peruvian teams.

We talked to Los Increibles before leaving, and thanked them for all of their help. We decided to give them our raft building tools. I later learned that the top three Peruvian teams are all cousins. Prior to this year, they had swept the awards and split approximately $1,800 in prize money. That is about half a year's earnings for the average Peruvian in Iquitos, so Easy Living's generosity was much appreciated.

We spent Sunday evening relaxing at our hotel. Dave and I walked down to an ice cream shop so I could finally satisfy my craving for some frozen treats. Anita was able to get her original passport returned to her after paying a small ransom to a "mediator" who represented the thief. Iquitos has a long way to go before it will became the safe, friendly tourist destination it is striving to be.

Early Monday morning we boarded our flight at Iquitos airport to begin our trip back to the States. Though we were coming home without any awards, I was happy with our team's performance. Despite a few setbacks, we had designed and built (with Incredible help) a competitive raft that we paddled to a fifth place finish in an international event. The raft race also enabled us to have a close-up view of life along the Amazon River that the typical tourist would miss.

Rod's TRAVELING TRIVIA

The Amazon River

The Amazon River is 3,980 miles in length, making it the second longest river in the world. It is the widest river on Earth, sometimes exceeding six miles. The Amazon accounts for 20 percent of the water flowing into the world's oceans. The volume of its water is greater than the next six rivers combined. The Amazon River collects water from streams and tributaries covering 40 percent of the South American continent. It flows through the countries of Peru and Brazil, before emptying into the Atlantic Ocean.

The first European discovered the Amazon when he was 200 miles out to sea, and noticed that he was sailing in fresh water. He turned his vessel towards

shore and found the massive river. To this day, ships still anchor in the outflow of the Amazon to remove saltwater barnacles. The river was named by Spanish explorer Francisco de Orellana. In 1541, while traveling the length of the river, Orellana and his men met a fierce tribe of women. They reminded him of a story from ancient Greece about female warriors known as Amazons.

Ye say they have all passed away,
that noble race and brave,

That their light canoes have vanished
from off the crystal wave;

That mid the forest where they roamed
there rings no hunter's shout,

But their name is on your waters,
and ye cannot wash it out.

—Unknown

Racing with Carl Poulsen in the
Wild Hog Canoe Race in 1986

In the Beginning...
the Early Years of Rod Enjoying
theThrill of Competition

Battling for position in the 1985 Wild Hog Canoe Race

Mike Gutierrez added a sailing rig to a racing canoe for speed and stability in the 2003 Everglades Challenge.

WaterTribe Everglades Challenge

2006 Everglades Challenge - Getting ready to launch from Fort DeSoto Park in Florida

My first "all day" race on the Suwannee River in 2002

The Suwannee River Challenge

The Big Shoals on the Suwannee River - White Springs, FL

Alafia Challenge Canoe Race with Ken Streb - Brandon, FL

Chelsea and I decorate a canoe at the Great
Dock Canoe Race in Naples, Florida

The pristine Wekiva River near Orlando, Florida.

Rod's Canoeing Sanctuary

Training on the Wekiva River has physical and mental benefits.

The pack takes off at the 2005 Adirondack

Adirondack Canoe Classic

Racing with Ken Streb in the 2005
Adirondack Canoe Classic

Ken carried the
canoe while I tried
to keep up

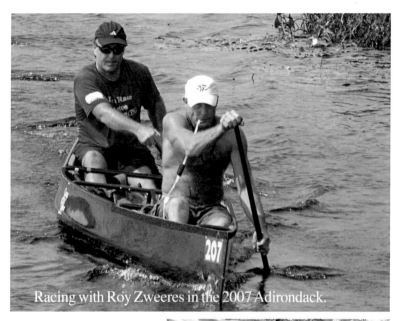

Racing with Roy Zweeres in the 2007 Adirondack.

Cramping up
at the end of
day one.

The jug of beer helped to
commemorate our win.

My first boat building experience with the
Chesapeake Lightcraft Company's triple kayak.

Building the "Condor"

Master boat builder, Marty Sullivan made the project much easier.

Applying a protective coat of epoxy

The Condor is launched in preparation for
the 2006 Everglades Challenge.

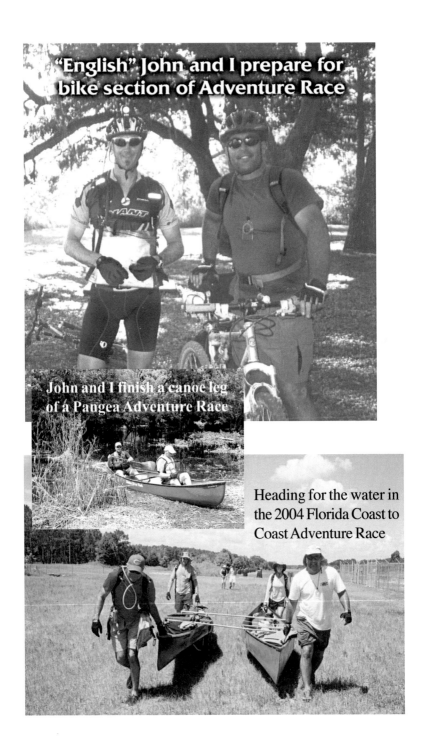

"English" John and I prepare for bike section of Adventure Race

John and I finish a canoe leg of a Pangea Adventure Race

Heading for the water in the 2004 Florida Coast to Coast Adventure Race

Coming in to the finish at Steinhatchee, FL in the 2006 Coast to Coast Adventure Race.

Florida Adventure Racing

Celebrating a successful race at the Coast to Coast

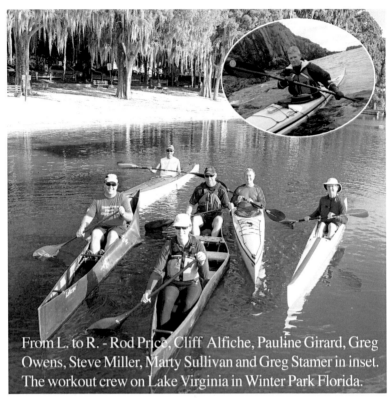

From L. to R. - Rod Price, Cliff Alfiche, Pauline Girard, Greg
Owens, Steve Miller, Marty Sullivan and Greg Stamer in inset.
The workout crew on Lake Virginia in Winter Park Florida.

The author laboring away.

Honing my machete skills

These guys are going down!

The Great Amazon Raft Race

The Florida Four with team Los Increibles

The Florida Four: Greg Talik, Anita Allen, Rod Price,
Dave Knothe indulge in some face painting

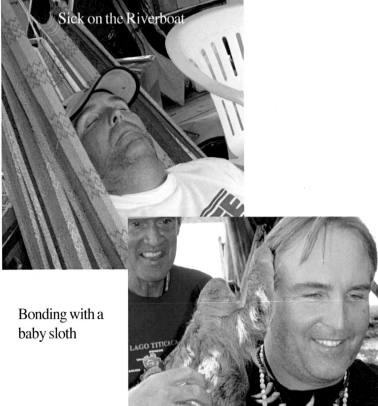

Sick on the Riverboat

Bonding with a
baby sloth

This craft is a little small for me

One of the tough Peruvian teams

Getting ready for the start of the raft race.

The Florida Four paddling towards Iquitos, Peru
on day three of the Great Amazon Raft Race.

CHAPTER 8

Are You Sure
You Want To Do This?

It was around October of 2008, that I first heard about the Yukon 1000 Canoe Race on one of the paddling websites I occasionally monitor. I had to laugh at the bold headline on the official race website, "Are you sure you want to do this?" I was not sure. For over a month, I thought about what would be involved in doing a race of this magnitude. I had to ask myself and prospective partners the following questions:

1. Was I willing to spend seven to ten days racing in a canoe?
2. Was I able to take time off from work (two weeks) to do the race?
3. Was I willing and able to spend $3,000 to do the race?
4. Was I willing and able to devote the training time needed for the race?

My answers were a resounding yes to all of the questions. After thirty years of canoe racing, this would be my ultimate challenge: one thousand miles on the historic Yukon River through the vast wilderness of Western Canada and Alaska. This would be more than three times longer than the 300 mile Everglades Challenge. Now, I needed to find a partner.

I contacted five or six racers by email, phone or in person about the Yukon race. All of them said yes to question #1, but questions #2 and #3 stopped them. Actually, in one case the wife killed the idea.

At some point I thought of Ardie Olson, and I'm glad I did. I first met Ardie at the Suwannee River Challenge in 2004. I later saw him at some of the high-profile adventure races in Florida. Ardie was captain and navigator of the "Mighty Dog" adventure racing team from the Atlanta, GA. area. In 2006, his team traveled all over the country winning races, and completed the Primal Quest Adventure Race in 10 days of continuous racing. By the end of the year, they had amassed enough points to win the U.S. Adventure Racing Association's national championship. In the last two years, Ardie had competed in the 2,700 mile Great Divide Bicycle Race, the 265 mile Texas Water Safari and was the first paddler to complete Alabama's 630 mile scenic canoe trail. At the age of 47, he was not slowing down.

I first emailed Ardie on Dec. 2, about the race, and a week later he said he was on board. Wow! I was going to be doing the world's longest canoe race on the Yukon River.

From that point on, the race was never far from my thoughts. Now there was the not so small matters of logistics and training. Fortunately, Ardie and Sherry, his talented wife, handled all of the logistics. They were in close contact with the race organizer, Peter Coates in Whitehorse, Yukon Territory of Canada. This was a first-year event, and Coates was working through the issues that come with such an ambitious race. He had to get approval for the race from multiple government agencies in two different countries.

For me, it was all about training. How does someone prepare for a 1,000 mile canoe race? I was asked this quite often over the next seven months. My first reaction was to avoid spending too much time in the canoe. It would be easy to suffer an "over-use" injury that would threaten my performance in the race. Therefore, my goal was to further strengthen my paddling foundation, and be injury-free at race time.

In January 2009, I decided to return to the 300-mile Everglades Challenge with Ardie as my partner. It would be my third time doing the race, and Ardie's first. More importantly, it gave us a major competition to focus on for the next two months. Ardie and I had never raced together, and this tough event would be a good "get to know you" race. We opted to use the Condor, the wooden, triple kayak that Marty Sullivan and I built and used in the 2006 race. With the race starting on March 7th, I had to rapidly boost my paddling hours. Ardie and I did two long training runs together on the Everglades route. The first went from Placida to Everglades City. Our first time in the boat went very well. Ardie came well-prepared with the maps and charts we needed. The run took close to 24 hours.

A couple of weeks later, we drove down to Everglades City for a more demanding excursion. Ardie and Sherry picked me up in Orlando Friday afternoon, and we arrived in time to have a nice seafood dinner in Everglades City. We had a good night's rest in the cabin we rented, and were up at 6 am to get ready for our paddle. By 7 am we were ready to leave, and told Sherry we would see her in Flamingo. From Everglades City we paddled south to the smaller town of Chokoloskee, a checkpoint for the race. Ardie and I kept going until we reached open water beyond the Everglades. I put up a V-shaped spirit sail to take advantage of the wind at our backs. With the sail and a strong paddling pace, our speed stayed around seven miles per hour. We still had over an hour of daylight left when we re-entered the Everglades for the shortcut to Flamingo. We paddled across Whitewater Bay, and Ardie's navigation lead us straight to the eight-mile canal to Flamingo. Sherry had a campsite and tent set up when we arrived. The local store was still open, and I had a nice chicken sandwich. The next morning we were again ready to paddle at 7 am. And again, we enjoyed ideal weather conditions. Ardie and I cruised into Key Largo in 8 1/2 hours. I felt we were in good shape for the Challenge.

The next few weeks went by quickly with regular paddling sessions and work, but I did manage to add another coat of epoxy to the triple kayak. Wooden boats are beautiful, but they also require more maintenance.

CHAPTER 9

Everglades Challenge 2009

Ardie and I were in Ft. DeSoto Park Friday afternoon for the paddlers' meeting. There were 52 people entered in the race on 34 different teams. Most of the teams were comprised of one or two racers. There was one six-person team racing in an Hawaiian-style outrigger equipped with a sail. The gear check-in went smoothly, and we listened attentively as the race director went over the rules. Not much had changed from the last time I was here three years ago. After the meeting, we went to dinner, and then returned to our hotel to make some adjustments to the kayak. Ardie would be sitting in the front of the kayak, which meant he would be controlling the rudder. I liked this arrangement. I needed only to concentrate on paddling hard, and not on steering.

Our alarm beeped at 5 am. Saturday morning, and we were soon on our way to breakfast. I stuffed myself with pancakes smothered in syrup and several helpings of eggs and bacon. It would be several days before I would have a decent meal again - might as well enjoy it.

We arrived at Ft. DeSoto Park, and immediately started moving our gear to the beach. It was still dark, and you could see the headlights of the other paddlers preparing their boats for the demanding voyage to Key Largo. Shortly after 7 am, the signal was given, and we were off. The winds were light,

but the forecasts were for increasing headwinds.
Ardie and I had a goal of finishing the race in under
three days. Other than sailboats, that had never
been done in the nine-year history of the event.
We headed straight across the channel entering
Tampa Bay aiming for the Intra Coastal Waterway.
Ardie and I could see a few of the sailboats angling
towards the Gulf. Our focus was on winning our
division, but beating a few sailboats to Key Largo
would be even better. As we headed down the Intra
Coastal, south of St. Petersburg, we maintained a
strong pace. After five hours of paddling, I could
not see any paddlers behind us. Ardie and I pulled
up to the Placida checkpoint after 8 pm. Four
sailboats had clocked in ahead of us, but we were
the first paddle craft to come in. We filled two of
our water jugs, and quickly left. Crossing Pine Island
Sound, we encountered more headwinds and waves.
I was getting soaked by the water blowing onto me
from Ardie's kayak paddle. I tightened the hood of
my rain jacket, and kept paddling. If this kept up,
we could forget about the three day record. The
constant up and down movement of the kayak's
rudder was causing it to bend to one side. By the
time we stopped in Sanibel Island around 5 am the
rudder was ready to fall off from metal fatigue. I
slept about an hour, while Ardie tried to repair the
rudder. Unfortunately, we had not brought a
welding torch or a spare rudder. When we starting
paddling again, it was clear I would need to do the
steering with my canoe paddle.

Ardie and I left Sanibel at 7 am. We were several
miles from the west coast of Florida, and still
battling waves and a persistent headwind. As we
headed south to Marco Island, I started

maneuvering the kayak closer to shore. I was hoping to find some calmer water, but there was no let-up in the wind. At this point, we were only going two to three miles per hour. I noticed that a couple walking on the beach was going faster than us. My only consolation was that everyone in the race was facing these conditions. Ardie and I made it to Marco Island in the early evening. Just south of the island we turned into a waterway that would lead us to Everglades City. We were relieved to be out of the wind, and took a ten-minute food break to celebrate. It was time for Ardie to navigate again, and he pulled out the charts he needed to guide us through the mangrove islands. About three in the morning, with both of us fighting the "sleep monsters," we found a nice beach on a small island to pull the kayak onto. I noticed our beleaguered rudder had fallen completely off. I would have no problem steering for the remainder of the race. We grabbed our tents and sleeping bags, and were quickly asleep. After two hours, Ardie's watch alarm went off and it was time to paddle again. We emerged from our tents to see that the tide had gone out while we slept. Ardie and I had to drag our heavily laden kayak 100 feet through the mud to find some deeper water. We were soon underway again. Despite some tricky navigation through the mangrove islands, we made good progress. Ardie and I went by Everglades City at 1:30 pm., and arrived at Chokoloskee at 3 pm. It was low tide however, and the kayak grounded-out about 60 feet from shore. We had to trudge through thick claylike muck to get to solid land. The Chokoloskee checkpoint always boosts my spirits because it is 174 miles into the race and over the halfway mark.

There is also a convenience store there, and it was refreshing to get a cold drink and a pre-made sandwich. I was already tired of eating my assortment of race food. We were further elated to learn that we were now running in second place overall, and had a big lead on the paddle craft behind us. The headwinds were obviously slowing everyone down. After a wonderful thirty minute break, we were ready to head east to Flamingo. Ardie and I soon reached open water again, and it was time to fight the headwinds. This was certainly tougher than our practice run. It was after nightfall when we made it to our entry point in the Everglades. Although navigation is much more difficult at night, Ardie lead us right to the Flamingo canal. We clocked into the Flamingo checkpoint a little before 3:30 am., still in second place overall.

Ardie and I moved our kayak and gear around the lock, and got into our sleeping bags for some more rest. At 7 am, the kayak was loaded, and we were off on the last leg of the race. Only 33 miles to go - what could go wrong? Well, to begin with, the wind was soon blowing stronger than ever. Ardie and I had to paddle hard just to make two miles per hour. After a couple hours of this, Ardie said his GPS unit had stopped working. Now he was relying on charts alone to guide us around the small islands. We kept heading east, and could soon see Key Largo. One wrong turn later, and we encountered the dreaded "mud berm" that Mike and I were mired in during the 2003 race. Fortunately, we hit it in the daylight, and managed to drag our kayak through a narrow section of the berm on the north side. Ardie and I now had a straight shot into Key Largo, but the island is miles long, and we were not sure which direction to head. We were looking for a cell phone tower that was the landmark for the finish. We could see four of the towers spreadout along the coast. Ardie wanted to head south, I was thinking north. We decided to paddle straight in to find out our exact location. Ardie soon spotted a concrete tower way to the north, and realized we were too far south. We now made a bee-line for the right cell phone tower, and thirty minutes later, pulled into the finish. Ardie was disappointed with his navigation mistakes, but I assured him they were minor compared to what I'd been through in 2003.

We had won our division with a final time of 3 days, 11 hours, 55 minutes. We held onto our second overall position, and beat the next paddle boat by 22 hours. It was a tough race that elevated our fitness to the level we would need for the Yukon 1000. Ardie and I won this race by being disciplined. We fought the wind and waves day after day, and despite being exhausted and sleep deprived, stayed with our race plan. I was very satisfied with our performance.

Back in Orlando, I continued my canoe workouts. I had committed to do a 30-hour adventure race in April, so I was also doing a lot of leg exercises - treadmill and biking. My two teammates in the adventure race were excellent racers, and I did not want to be the "weak" link.

2009 Atlantic Coast Conquest Adventure Race

A 24 hour or longer adventure race is a demanding test of an athlete's physical and mental fitness. To be continuously moving by foot, bicycle or canoe for over a day is a tough challenge. A challenge like this can only help prepare me for the Yukon 1000.

The Atlantic Coast Conquest Adventure Race is one of the premier adventure racing events in Central Florida. Teams ranging from two to four persons have up to thirty hours to complete a demanding course through the Florida wilderness. Each team has a navigator who uses maps and a compass to lead his team from one checkpoint to the other. Each checkpoint is designated by an orange and white flag with its own hand-punch that racers use on a passport to prove they found it. In 2008, John Hollingsworth and I won the ACC to capture our biggest adventure race win. John could not make this year's race.

On Saturday, April 18th, I was on the starting line with my two teammates, Ron Eaglin and Allen McAdams, for the ACC 30-Hour Adventure Race. Dr. Ron Eaglin, 46, is a professor at the University of Central Florida in Orlando. In 2008, he led his team to an impressive 18th place finish in the two-week long Primal Quest adventure race. Allen McAdams, 43, is also an elite adventure racer, and has frequently raced with Ardie Olson. Team Eco-Choice, my former business name, with a different line-up, was back to defend our ACC title. The race was being held at St. Augustine, Florida. We had arrived Friday evening for the pre-race meeting and to receive our course maps. Ron was our navigator, and with 44 checkpoints to find - he was going to be very busy.

To start the race, we were given a choice of doing a bike or a trekking section. We decided to trek first, bike second. Ron had twisted his ankle the previous weekend at an orienteering competition. It slowed him down enough to where I could keep up with his pace. Allen coaches a track team in Georgia, and can run like a deer. The trekking leg took about 90 minutes to find five checkpoints. The following bike leg went equally well, and we arrived back at the transition area within five minutes of the leaders. Next was the paddle leg on the Intra Coastal Waterway. There were three of us in one canoe. Allen was in the front, Ron in the middle and I was steering from the rear. We paddled about ten miles south to Stoke's Landing, where we beached our canoe for a short trekking section of four checkpoints. The first three points were somewhat easy to find, but checkpoint 21 was a big problem. We kept running into wide fire breaks that were cut in the forest, and not shown on our maps. Ron finally had us loop around towards the river, and after close to an hour - we found it. We then returned to the canoe, with me shuffling along in the back.

I was happy to be getting back in the canoe. Ron discovered a shortcut to the main channel that saved us at least 20 minutes. We found a few more checkpoints on the return trip. When we reached the transition zone again, we found out that team

Eco-Choice was still in the top five. We set out on our bikes as darkness was beginning to fall. There would be no more canoe legs in the race. I was not looking forward to 18 hours of biking and trekking. The bike leg had a total of 16 checkpoints. The section started well, with Ron leading us to point after checkpoint. Then came the major problem, checkpoint 30. What made it more frustrating was that we spotted the orange and white checkpoint marker during the paddling section. At one point, we were with five or six other teams looking for CP 30. When an hour went by without finding it, we decided to skip it - hoping the other teams were having the same trouble. Shortly before 6 am, we started the final trek. I told Ron and Allen that my legs were done; meaning that a fast walking pace was about it. We did not have any trouble finding the remaining six markers. As usual with the arrival of daylight, I received a nice jolt of energy. My legs felt good during the eight-mile bike leg to end the race. Team Eco-Choice crossed the finish line around 10 am in sixth place in the elite division. The top four teams managed to find CP 30. We gave it our best, but sometimes that is not good enough. I enjoyed racing with Ron and Allen, it is clear to me why they are among the best adventure racers in the southeast.

After a long adventure race, I usually take a few days off from working-out to give my mind and body a chance to recover. My leg muscles were very sore following the ACC. By Thursday, I was back on the water for a two-hour canoe training session. On the weekends, my goal was to do one seven to eight-hour workout. I would usually put-in on the St. Johns River and paddle a mile to the smaller Wekiva

River. From there I would paddle 18 miles against the current to the springhead at Wekiva Springs State Park. I would take a break at the Park, refill a water bottle, and paddle back down to the St. Johns. This was my training schedule through the end of May.

In June, Ardie and I met on the Suwannee River for a long training run. We started in Fargo, GA. at 7 am. Saturday morning. The water level was about four feet above average on the Suwannee, which helped our progress down the river. Around 2 pm, we were nearing the class III rapids known as Big Shoals. Some canoers had flipped their overloaded canoe above the Shoals, and we towed one of their heavy coolers to shore for them. At the portage for the rapids, we carried our gear down the trail. Ardie then demonstrated his whitewater skills by easily running the rapids while seated in the middle of the canoe. We loaded-up again, and were soon heading towards White Springs. Ardie and I saw a half-sunken canoe down from the Shoals. As we approached it, we noticed a man about 100 yards downriver on the shore. After some yelling back and forth, we determined it was his canoe, and proceeded to tow it down to him. He thanked us, and said he was waiting for his buddy who was paddling a kayak. It was definitely amateur day on the Suwannee River. Being careless in a small boat can easily lead to tragedy.

Ardie and I continued downriver in the nicely flowing current. We made good progress for the remainder of the day. Towards nightfall, we found a sand bar suitable for camping. I brought a brand new one-man tent I planned to use during the Yukon race. After setting it up, and squeezing into it with my sleeping bag, I was pretty cramped. I couldn't even sit-up in this tent without pulling the tent stakes out of the ground. For the Yukon race, if the weather or bugs were bad, I might be spending a lot of time in my tent. I had a two-man tent I would try out on our next trip - even if it was a little heavier.

Ardie set his watch alarm for 5 am, and we were back on the river by 6 am. It started to rain off and on by 10 am, so we put on our rain jackets. We were fortunate not to encounter any lightning storms. Ardie and I arrived in Branford, FL about 2:30 pm. Wendall from American Canoe Adventures was waiting to shuttle us back to our vehicles. We had covered 140 miles, not a bad workout. I wondered what kind of mileage our competition was putting in.

The next weekend I drove up to Ardie and Sherry's house in north Georgia for the "Back to the Chattahoochee" Canoe Race in Roswell. The course is less than 10 miles long, but it is one of the best attended races in the Southeast. This was my fourth time entering the race, and hopefully it would be my fourth victory. I brought my 18 1/2 ft. carbon fiber tandem racing canoe. It was a little banged-up from use in adventure races, but still a fast canoe. Last year I had won this race with Allen McAdams, my adventure racing teammate. This year Allen was racing with Paul Cox, another adventure racer, in a woodstrip racing canoe. Lightweight woodstrip canoes were used by racers before Kevlar® and carbon fiber became the preferred materials. Ardie and I had never paddled together in my racing canoe, and we were lucky not to flip after the race started. A racing canoe is much more unstable than a recreational canoe. It was about ten minutes into the race before I was feeling comfortable. We were in the lead, but Allen and Paul were right behind us. I was slowly moving my seat forward to balance the canoe, and help us run more efficiently. Not wanting to alert our competition, I quietly told Ardie to pick up the pace. We slowly started to pull away. Near the halfway point there are some class II rapids that have caused me some anxiety in past years. A racing canoe is designed for "flatwater," and it would be easy to have problems in this section. Ardie was familiar with the rapids however, and with his positioning - we made it through cleanly.

Once clear of the rapids, I looked back and did not see Allen and Paul. After the race, we learned that they had cracked there wooden canoe on a rock going through the rapids. Ardie and I cruised to the finish line in first place. After having a quick snack, Sherry shuttled us back to the starting line so we could run the course again. The second time was much more enjoyable, and we easily cleared the rapids again. We arrived back in time to receive our first place awards. Team Olson and Price was now two for two in races. On Sunday morning, Ardie and I paddled 20 miles on Lake Lanier in North Georgia. We then went out for a nice lunch, and it was time for me to head home to Orlando.

On Saturday, June 21st, I was competing in the six-hour Seminole County Adventure Race (SCAR) northeast of Orlando. My usual adventure race partner, John Hollingsworth and I were racing in the elite division. There is a much faster pace in a six-hour race compared to a 30-hour event. With all of the paddling I was doing, my legs had been a little neglected since the ACC race. Two hours into the race, the Central Florida heat was taking its toll. I was drinking plenty of liquids, and taking electrolite supplements to avoid muscle cramping, but my energy level had plummeted. John and I finished the canoe leg of the race in fourth position, and then set-out on a "mud walk" through the forest to find six more checkpoints. When we were ready to start the final bike section, my body was "running on empty." I mostly just followed John as we picked-off the last few check-points. As we approached the six-hour time limit, we decided to give up on the last checkpoint. John and I were heading out of the woods when I spotted the last orange and white marker in an unexpected location. Sometimes its better to be lucky than good. Team Eco-Choice finished in eighth position out of 28 teams, but I felt fortunate just to finish the race.

The next weekend Ardie and I did another training run on the Suwannee River. This time it was not overcast, and the river current had slowed. It was incredibly hot by the early afternoon. Ardie said his watch thermometer read 100 degrees. We took a thirty minute break to cool down in one of the springs that empty into the Suwannee. By early evening we had made it to Suwannee River State Park. I hiked up to the facilities building, and returned with four cold sodas from the drink machine. That was the highlight of my day. We camped on a point of land where the Withlacoochee River flows into the Suwannee. I had made a point of taking a two-man tent. I was much more comfortable in this spacious shelter. On Sunday we paddled about five miles up the Withlacoochee. Ardie and I encountered several sets of rapids, one of which required us to get out and drag the canoe through the strong current. We soon turned around, and paddled back to the Suwannee. Our shuttle service picked us up at the state park shortly after midday. Back in White Springs, I said goodbye to Ardie and told him I would see him next month in Canada.

Over the next three weeks I stayed on my training program which included two 40-mile workouts on the St. Johns and Wekiva Rivers in the intense Florida heat. I had my last two-hour workout on Thursday morning, and that evening I met eight of my friends and training partners at a restaurant for a send-off dinner. They all said they would be watching the race on the internet. I hoped Ardie and I would be prepared for the challenges of the Yukon 1000.

Going the Distance
The Yukon 1000 mile Canoe Race

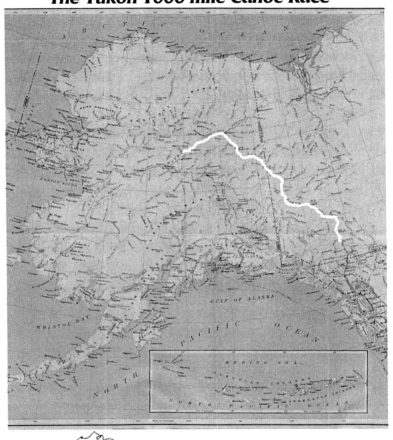

Alaska

A comparison of the
size of Alaska relative
to the State of Florida

CHAPTER 11

Thoughts on the Yukon

Well, the big day arrived. I was sitting in the airliner awaiting takeoff, bound for the Yukon. I estimate that I have probably competed in about 400 canoe related races of all types and distances in my life. This one was different in many ways. The distance was 1,000 miles, which makes it by far the longest race. It will be an odd feeling to hit the 500 mile mark, and only be halfway finished. The race organizer expects the fast teams to cover over 160 miles a day. The seven to eight mile-per-hour current in the Yukon will give us a nice push. On the first day of the race we will cross Lake LaBerge. This is a large body of water stretching over 30 miles long with very little current. This crossing should be the first indicator as to who the strongest teams are. It would be nice to be the first canoe leaving the lake and picking up the fast current of the Yukon River again. There are some class I and II rapids on the river that will demand our attention. Rapids are rated by their severity from the easiest - class I, to the toughest - class VI. Our canoe has a spray skirt that will hopefully be effective. In the 460 mile Yukon River Quest, a couple of racers flip each year. That canoe and kayak race runs from Whitehorse to Dawson City, almost the halfway point for us. This is the point when the serious contenders should be asserting themselves. Ardie and I should be among the strongest; particularly in the second half of the race. We are used to pushing ourselves in long races, and know how to maintain a good pace.

We will definitely be at our most vulnerable when we are camping. I have heard the biting flies and mosquitoes are ferocious. My main concerns are bears and moose. Getting mauled by a one-ton Grizzly would absolutely spoil my race. The old joke about not having to outrun the bear – only your partner, doesn't help either. Ardie is the faster runner...

Each team is required to find a campsite around 11 pm, and cannot start paddling again for six hours. We will have a Spot tracking device that monitors our movement by satellite. It will be important to stay disciplined in the "down" time. One hour to set-up tents, eat and drink, apply recovery aids (pain relievers, ointments, sports cream). Four hours to sleep – hopefully a sound, restful sleep. And then one hour to break camp, re-pack the canoe, eat breakfast and prepare for 18 more hours of paddling. As required, Ardie has a water filter we will be using throughout the race. We will obviously need to manage our water intake, especially if the warmer temperatures persist in the area.

While conditioning is important in a multi-day race, it is the ability to tolerate your increasing discomfort as the competition progresses that often determines the victor. In other words, you need to be able to "out suffer" the other competitors. Instead of focusing on how miserable you feel, use the pain to push yourself towards the finish line. Ardie has a great term for a race like this - a "sufferfest."

CHAPTER 12

Journey to Whitehorse

I arrived in Whitehorse at 7:30 pm Pacific Standard Time. It had been a long day of airport lines, security screenings, layovers, takeoffs and landings. From Orlando, I flew to Los Angeles, then to Vancouver and now at last to Whitehorse, Yukon Territory - Canada. I was happy to see Ardie and Sherry Olson in the main terminal. I was also happy to see my checked bag and paddle box on the luggage conveyor. The night before leaving, I made a cardboard box to hold my three carbon fiber paddles. Each paddle is about 50 inches long and weighs less than a pound. Two of the paddles are nine inches wide, the third is eight and a half. In racing circles, a nine inch blade is unusual because of the increased effort it takes to move a paddle that size through the water. I have been using a wide blade for several years with excellent results. I can handle the increased torque, and the extra power that is generated by each stroke is a nice edge to have over the competition. I brought the narrower paddle in case I am struggling in the last few days of the race.

Ardie and Sherry arrived two days earlier in Whitehorse. After dropping my things at the Yukon Inn, we headed out for dinner. They led me to the Klondike Rib and Salmon BBQ Restaurant. The structure was built in 1900, and has housed an auto parts company and Klondike Airlines.

Following an excellent meal, we strolled a few blocks down to the Yukon River. My first impression of the river was one of concern. Watching from the shore, the current was really cranking. If we flipped in this, it would be a very difficult to get our water-laden canoe to shore. I kept my thoughts to myself. We spent the rest of the evening looking in the various shops in downtown Whitehorse.

On Saturday morning we drove over to Peter Coates' house to take our first look at the canoe we have rented for the race. I have heard a few stories over the years about racers renting boats, and being stuck with a vessel that was barely sea worthy. For the Yukon race, the only sensible option was to rent a canoe. It would have cost around $2,000. to ship a canoe to Whitehorse. Also, there are not too many canoes in Florida that are equipped with spray skirts for whitewater. We saw our blue colored canoe in the front yard, and after closely inspecting it - were pleased with its condition. This was definitely a canoe we could win the race with. Made of Kevlar® and Jensen designed, it would be as fast as any canoe in the race. We left the canoe with Coates, not wanting to risk it being stolen from the hotel.

The next item on the agenda was food. We were required to carry 20 kilograms of food per paddler, which for the metrically challenged is 44 lbs. That was a lot of food. As a precaution against bad weather, Coates wants us to have enough food for three weeks in the Yukon wilderness.

You might think a couple of serious athletes like ourselves would have a carefully chosen list of foods for an undertaking like this. Actually it is all about personal preference. I looked for food that has plenty of calories, will digest well and tastes good. My selection definitely reflects my sweet tooth. I picked a box of mini-carrot cakes, some chocolate crispy treats and two boxes of pop tarts. I was disappointed that I could not find any cinnamon-frosted pop tarts in all of Whitehorse, so I settled for strawberry and blueberry. I also added a box of chocolate chip cookies, two cans of Pringles potato chips, a bag of apples (mostly for the weight) and a few bananas. Ardie advised me to add some protein. On his recommendation, I bought a bag of twenty-foot long pepperoni sticks and some packets of cheese. I brought two containers of turkey jerky and an assortment of about 60 snack bars from Florida. I had about 20 packets of energy and protein powder mixes, along with some servings of oatmeal. Our next stop was a camping store where I found a wide variety of freeze-dried meals. I picked a few pasta meals, and threw in a couple of breakfast entrees.

Now I needed to find a bear canister to protect my food from all the critters - large and small. The canister is made of hardened plastic with a screw-top lid that locks into place. It was difficult for people to open it, and supposedly impossible for bears. Although, there was a report of a black bear in New York learning to open one. Hopefully that information will not make it to the Yukon anytime soon. I found a suitable canister at a local canoe outfitter. I also decided to buy some "bear spray." This is designed to act as a repellent to bears if deployed accurately. I doubt my accuracy would be very good if I was being mauled to death by a big Grizzly bear. Ardie decided not to buy any spray, so maybe a few squirts of the spray would at least send the bear in his direction. Just kidding, of course!

For dinner, we had a very poor meal at a well-known pizza chain. Too bad it was my choice. We then went back to the hotel to watch some TV before retiring.

Sunday morning I was a little late getting up, as the symptoms of a sinus infection were starting to appear. Ardie and Sherry decided to head over to Coates' house to retrieve the canoe while I got ready. We planned to take a practice run on the Yukon this afternoon. They returned with the boat, and we had a good breakfast at the hotel. Ardie and I then loaded all of our food and equipment into the car, and drove down to the river for the gear check-in. Coates was ready for us when we got there. First Ardie, and then I stood on the weight scale. The weights were recorded, and we then grabbed our bags of food and were weighed again. I hit the 44 lb. mark on the first try. It must have been the bag of apples. Ardie was a couple of pounds short, and added some food he had left in the car. The rest of the inspection went smoothly as we showed Coates the following items: tents, sleeping bags, mini-stove, fuel, flashlights, waterproof matches, knife, whistle, warm clothing, bear canisters, water filter, life-preservers, and a signaling mirror. One other curious item we had to carry was a piece of aluminum foil to put on our heads so large boats on the river would see us on their radar. Since we are not paddling in darkness, I doubted we would need our tin foil hats.

Sherry, Ardie and I then walked down to a pavilion by the river for the pre-race briefing. It was interesting to observe the group of about 40 paddlers who were taking on the world's longest river race. Their ages ranged from 21 to 65. There were five female racers. It is tough to guess who the serious challengers will be. To get in the race, everybody had to demonstrate to Coates that their wilderness and, or racing background was adequate for this event. A few of the racers have done the 460 mile Yukon River Quest before.

The focus of the briefing was the Satellite Personal Tracker (SPOT). This device allows users to send messages from areas without any cell phone coverage. In an emergency the panic button can be pushed, and a signal would be sent to the authorities. Coates makes it clear that it had better be a real crisis before the button is pushed - "like your head has been ripped-off by a bear." During the race each team was required to hit the "okay" button on the SPOT every six hours. When we stopped to camp the button was to be pushed. In the morning, when we started moving again the button was also pushed. This allowed Coates and the rest of the Internet world to monitor the progress of the race. People that were thousands of miles away from the Yukon would know more about our placement in the race than we will. Coates' stressed that teams failing to properly use the SPOT will be subject to penalties and even disqualification. I was confident in Ardie's ability to follow the SPOT rules to the letter, but I was also uneasy about relying so heavily on technology. I told Ardie that if we were unfairly penalized, and it costs us a win - I was going to throw Coates' ass in the river!

Following the meeting, Ardie and I were ready to gain a little Yukon River experience. We unloaded the canoe, and put a few water jugs behind Ardie's seat to balance us out. We said goodbye to Sherry, and off we went. After a few minutes of adjusting to the fast current, I settled into a comfortable pace. As we left Whitehorse behind us, I started to appreciate the beautiful scenery of the area. What started as a crazy thought was now a reality. I was paddling a canoe on the Yukon River. Ardie and I kept up a good pace for about an hour and twenty minutes. We soon noticed Sherry on the left bank signaling our take-out near the Takhini River. The short workout went a long way towards building my confidence for the race. After loading up the canoe, we drove back to the hotel. We played it safe, and had dinner at the Yukon Inn. We spent the rest of the evening sorting gear into our various dry bags. I climbed into bed at 10 pm. Tomorrow night's sleeping arrangements will be radically different.

Sourtoe Cocktail Club

In the 1920s, Louie and Otto Liken made their living hauling rum with sled-dog teams from Canada to Alaska. During one trip, Louie got his foot wet. Fearing that the Northwest Mounted Police were on their trail, they did not stop, and poor Louie's big toe froze. Once safely back at their cabin, Louie realized that the toe would need to be amputated to avoid gangrene. The brothers consumed enough of their 180% overproof rum to be sufficiently inebriated, and Otto cut off Louie's toe with one swing of his axe. The brothers decided to keep the toe in a jar of alcohol to remember the occasion.

Decades later, the toe was discovered in their cabin by Captain Dick Stevenson. After returning to Dawson City with the toe, Capt. Dick and his friends started the "Sourtoe Cocktail Club" in 1973 at the Eldorado Hotel. To join the club, your lips must touch the toe as you drink your favorite beverage.

In 1980, a gold miner named Garry Younger was trying to set a new Sourtoe record. On his thirteenth glass of Sourtoe champagne, his chair tipped over backwards, and he swallowed the toe. Sadly, the toe was never recovered. But soon another toe was donated, and the tradition still continues.

"YOU CAN DRINK IT FAST,
YOU CAN DRINK IT SLOW –

BUT THE LIPS HAVE GOTTA
TOUCH THE TOE."

DAY ONE

Ardie and I covered close to 90 miles on the first day. We didn't know it, but we had built a 20 mile lead on the second place canoe team, Dueling Banjos.

CHAPTER 13

DAY 1 - LAKE LABERGE

Race day finally arrived. After all of the preparation, it was exciting to be on the brink of starting this epic race. Unfortunately, I had come down with a sinus infection. I attributed that to the drier air than I was accustomed to in Florida. I stopped in at the local Whitehorse pharmacy and after consulting the pharmacist, bought the recommended medicine. Ardie, Sherry, and I had a good breakfast before heading to the river. There were a few teams already setting up when we arrived. Ardie and I started the race with four gallons of liquid. We each had over 40 lbs. of food as required by the rules. Add in our tents, sleeping bags, and extra clothes and we had a fully loaded canoe. I was over 40 lbs. heavier than Ardie, so the water jugs went right behind his seat to even things out. After loading the canoe, we went out for a test paddle and were still stern heavy. We needed to have the canoe evenly balanced so it would glide through the water more efficiently. Ardie slid his seat forward a few inches, and we moved more gear towards the front of the canoe. Now we were balanced.

Race time was approaching. The race was

scheduled to start at exactly 11 am. Two flags on either side of the Yukon River marked the starting line. Because of the fast current, teams had to estimate when to launch from the shore. You could try to get a running start, but there were time penalties for hitting the line early. I checked with Coates, and my watch was ten seconds faster than his. We were among the first canoes to launch, and crossed the starting line a few seconds after 11 am. The world's longest canoe race was officially under way. Our strategy was to take it out hard, and see who followed us. We took the lead in the canoe division very quickly. It seemed most of our competition was starting with a moderate pace. Did they know something we didn't?

There was a 24 ft. long, black carbon fiber Voyager class canoe with seven paddlers in it that did get a running start. We spent most of the first two hours trying to catch them. Although they were not in our class, drafting behind them would sure have saved us a lot of energy. I checked my watch as we passed the in-flowing Takhini River, and we were a few minutes faster than our practice run. In canoe and kayak racing it is legal to get right behind another boat and ride along in their slipstream, or wake. Wake riding can save a team 20 to 30 percent on their energy output. The seven-person Voyager canoe would have provided a nice ride for us. It soon became evident that their running speed was a little faster than ours. As we approached Lake

LaBerge, two tandem kayaks were in the lead, followed by the Voyager, and then us. I did not see any canoes behind us as we entered the lake. I told Ardie that this was a very good sign.

Lake LaBerge is approximately 30 miles long and two to three miles wide. We had a strong wind pushing us going into the lake, which meant the waves were getting bigger as we crossed. Ardie and I tightened our spray skirts around our waists. This was going to be a wild ride. Soon the waves were running two to three feet. We surfed on the top of the waves before plunging nose-first into the bottom of the next wave. My job was to keep the canoe "squared-up" to the waves. If we slid sideways into the trough of a wave, we could have easily flipped over. This type of paddling demanded all of our attention. There were moments when we had to paddle extremely hard to keep the canoe on course. We slowly headed towards the right side of the lake. If we were to capsize, at least we would have been closer to the shore. A third tandem kayak passed us on the lake. We were not concerned; it was only the canoes we were racing. After about four hours, we exited the lake – tired and relieved to be re-entering the fast moving Yukon. Ardie and I had passed the first test the race had thrown us.

We took five minutes to eat a snack, and were off again. After every long straight stretch of river, I looked behind us for any glimpse of our competition. I didn't see anyone. We soon went by the third place kayak again, and an hour later they passed us back. Because we started at 11 am, this would be one of our shortest paddling days. Around 10:30 pm, we started looking for a camping spot. We soon saw the Voyager crew setting-up camp on the left side of the river. Just past them, we checked a spot on the right side – but it was swampy. A few minutes later we found a suitable location on the left side. It had about a six-foot bank that we threw our gear up on. We set-up our tents among the trees on a nice bed of moss. The mosquitoes were buzzing, so I donned my head-net. I quickly threw my gear in the tent and climbed into my nylon sanctuary. I took off my damp shorts and shirt, and put on a comfy pair of sweatpants and a long-sleeve shirt. Whether it was from the sinus infection, hard paddling or a combination of both, I was exhausted. I am glad this was a 12 hour day instead of the 18 hour days we would be paddling the rest of the week. We agreed to skip a "hot" dinner. I ate a carrot cake snack and an apple, and quickly fell asleep.

Ardie estimated we had covered about 88 miles today. Lake LaBerge definitely slowed us down, but it probably had a worse affect on the other canoes. We seemed to have established a good lead on the rest of the canoe field. I was pleased with our performance on the first day. Let the sufferfest begin.

Rod's TRAVELING TRIVIA

Klondike Gold Rush

George Washington Carmack and two Indian friends, Tagish Charley and Shookum Jim are credited with igniting one of the largest gold rushes in history. On August 16, 1896, the group found a gold nugget in Rabbit Creek, a tributary of the Klondike River that empties into the Yukon River. The rest of the world caught Klondike gold fever the following July (1897) when 68 scraggly miners arrived at the docks in Seattle and San Francisco with more than two tons of gold. While millions of dollars worth of gold was pulled from the region in the ensuing years, the most compelling stories come from the estimated 100,000 people who quit their jobs, sold their possessions and set out on a very arduous journey to the area.

In Seattle, streetcar drivers left their trolleys, a quarter of the police force quit and even the mayor resigned to buy a steamboat to carry passengers to Alaska. The gold seekers were called "stampeders," and quickly overwhelmed the existing transportation options to get to the Yukon. The stampeders who made it to Alaska still had hundreds of miles to travel before arriving at the gold fields. Many were forced to turn back as they found the cost of hiring horses or mules to move their provisions to be too expensive. For the more determined Klondikers there were several trails to choose from. One of the trails, Dyea Trail, featured the infamous Chilkoot Pass - a severe, four mile long slope that was too steep for pack animals.

In the winter of 1897, over 20,000 would-be miners toiled night and day to move their loads over the pass; having to make the trek over and over with what they could carry on their backs. The Dyea Trail ended at Lake Bennett which feeds into the Yukon River. Here our poor stampeders spent the winter in tents waiting for the spring thaw, and constructing rafts to carry them down the Yukon River for 500 miles to the gold zone. For those whose craft withstood the rapids, the new gold boom town of Dawson City awaited. Here the final disappointment occurred when they found out that every gold-bearing creek in the region had been staked out. Most sold their gear and returned home at this point. A few found jobs in town or working on someone else's claim. The Klondike gold rush ended in 1899 when gold was discovered in Alaska. In one week 8,000 of Dawson City's 40,000 population left for Nome in August 1899.

DAY TWO

Five Finger Rapids provided some excitement for Ardie and I. We covered 171 miles today, and added another 12 miles to our lead over Dueling Banjos.

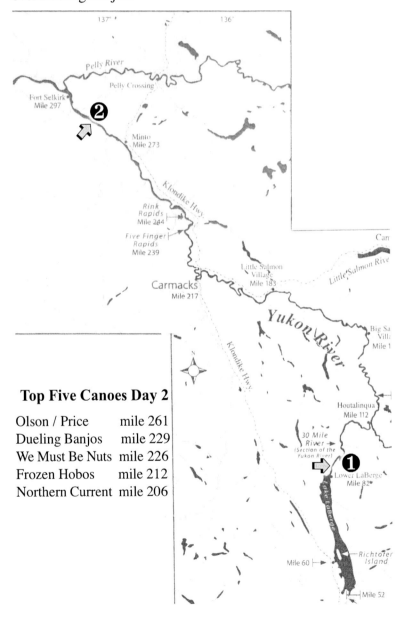

Top Five Canoes Day 2

Olson / Price	mile 261
Dueling Banjos	mile 229
We Must Be Nuts	mile 226
Frozen Hobos	mile 212
Northern Current	mile 206

CHAPTER 14

DAY 2 - FIVE FINGER RAPIDS

I was somewhat awake when Ardie yelled that it was time to get up. I felt pretty good. The time was 3:35 am, five hours since we had stopped. We wanted to be on the water in one hour. I began the ritual I would repeat each of the next six days. I rolled up my sleeping bag, and stuffed it back in its tiny bag. I changed back into my damp paddling clothes - not a great feeling. I put on a wind-breaker jacket, although the weather was quite mild in the morning. I removed my gear from the tent. As I broke down my tent, I noticed Ardie was already moving his gear towards the canoe. I stored the tent and poles in a large dry bag, with my sleeping bag. Now I was ready to load the canoe. We saw the Voyager come around the bend. We had ten minutes before the six hour mark. I was moving as fast as I could to mix-up a protein shake, and assemble my food supply of snack bars, turkey jerky and apples for the day. We left about ten minutes late. That could have easily meant a mile lost from our lead. I will have to move a little faster tomorrow morning.

As streams and rivers continued to pour into the Yukon, the river was now twice as wide as it was in Whitehorse. After about 30 minutes of paddling, we stopped to eat a light breakfast while the current kept us moving at close to five mph. Ardie and I limited our breaks to less than three minutes once or twice an hour. We wanted to maximize the time we spent paddling with the current. To the question of bathroom breaks; we had "pee" bottles that were used in our designated breaks.

We were soon underway again. Today's paddling focal points were the town of Carmacks and Five Finger Rapids. Carmacks was about 100 miles away. So it would be mid to late afternoon before we saw it. Ardie was expecting his wife, Sherry to be there. I was hoping she would have some information on the canoes behind us. We settled into a good pace, and the hours started to roll by. It warmed up quickly, and I took off my jacket. Ardie saw a Cinnamon Black Bear on the right bank. It was over a half mile away, and looked a lot smaller than it actually was. I hoped this would be as close as we got to bears in this race.

I had my watch attached to the spray skirt, so I was not tempted to look at it too often. Ardie and I had spent enough time together on long workouts and races, to have exhausted most of the "getting to know you" conversation. Occasionally, I would think of something interesting to say, but mostly it's just long periods of silence. By 3:00 pm, we were getting close to Carmacks. Ardie and I began to see scattered river cabins along the river, and an hour later arrived in the big city of Carmacks - population 426. We spotted Sherry and photographer Ron Bernardin on the right bank, and paddled towards them. Sherry said we were about 20 minutes behind the Voyager crew, but she wasn't sure how big our lead was over the second canoe. Ardie and Sherry exchanged their "love yous," and we were soon around the bend and heading for highlight number two – Five Finger Rapids.

Before the race, I was somewhat nervous about these rapids. Every year in the 460 mile Yukon River Quest, several racers flip over in the fast water. A capsized, loaded canoe is a big problem. It would be very hard to pull to shore, and important gear and food could be lost in the process. But after battling the waves on Lake LaBerge, I was comfortable with the handling of the canoe and looking forward to some excitement. About two and a half hours after passing Carmacks, Ardie informed me that Five Fingers was around the bend. The Five Fingers are giant basalt boulders scattered across the river, and churning-up the water. As we approached the rapid, we took a few minutes to secure our spray skirts. Sherry was watching us from an observation post on top of a "finger" on the right bank. Ardie was an old whitewater pro, and I told him not to be shy when giving instructions. The recommended route through the rapids was on the right side between fingers one and two. Paddlers needed to stay left of the standing waves to avoid the rocks. We quickly entered the rapid, and are being pulled towards the rocks. Ardie was yelling, "Left! Left!" I was paddling as hard as I could on the right side of the canoe to keep us away from the roughest water. After a few tense seconds we were through without a scratch. I could see how paddlers could easily get into trouble in these rapids. Down from the Fingers there was more disturbed water, but nothing to get excited about. Soon the river had calmed down, and we took a few minutes to eat and drink.

As evening progressed, the sun dipped down just enough to be a real nuisance. We were paddling straight into the sun, and with the light being reflected off the water, sunglasses were not much of a help. We were covering a lot of miles today, and Ardie was happy when we passed by the small town of Minto. He was not sure we would make it that far today. Ardie and I paddled for two more hours before it was time to find a camp site. There were plenty of low lying gravel and sand islands to choose from. We were in the area of the Yukon River known as Hell's Gate because it was a common spot for ships and barges to run aground over a century ago. We soon pulled-up on an island that suited us both.

Ardie preferred to set his tent up on gravel. I liked a smooth, sandy patch for mine. As we unloaded the canoe, I was amazed by how much better I felt than the previous day. And we paddled six more hours today. The sinus medicine I had been taking was working well. I used Ardie's water filter to fill two of our gallon jugs. At this point, the Yukon River was somewhat clean, and the process of pumping the water through the filter went smoothly. We both agreed to skip a hot dinner again. I munched on some pepperoni sticks, cookies and another apple. I then moved my food bag and bear canister about 20 ft. from the tent. Have at it animals, just let me get my four hours of sleep. We covered about 171 miles on day two, which turned out to be our most productive day. I was feeling confident as I lapsed into a deep sleep.

STERNWHEELERS

The S.S. Evelyn, a 130-foot sternwheeler built in 1908, rests on Shipyard Island. Its decaying structure can be seen through the trees from the Yukon River. The Evelyn carried supplies to trading posts along the river until 1918 when she was scrapped. The boiler of the Evelyn was installed at a Dawson City hotel in 1926 to provide power and hot water.

Sternwheelers first appeared on the Yukon River in 1866. Their steam powered paddle-wheels were fueled by wood. It took about 120 cords of wood for the 460 mile trip from Whitehorse to Dawson. There are still remnants of the wood camps that were set up along the river to supply the vessels. Some of the sternwheelers could carry up to 250 tons of cargo.

All-weather roads, railroads and airplanes eventually made the sternwheelers obsolete. Two of the riverboats have been preserved along the Yukon River. The S.S. Klondike can be found in Whitehorse, and the S.S. Keno in Dawson City.

DAY THREE

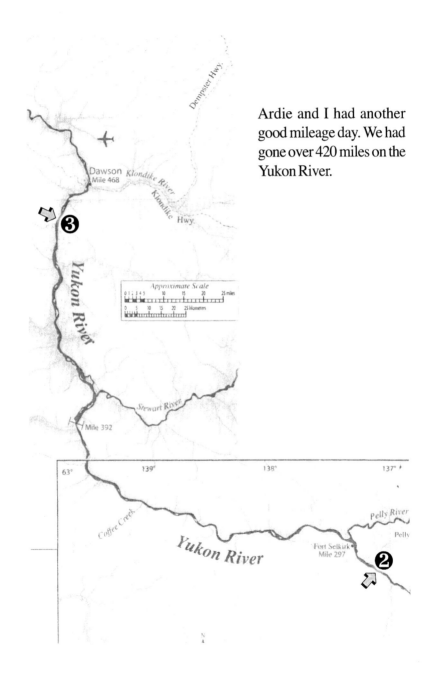

Ardie and I had another good mileage day. We had gone over 420 miles on the Yukon River.

CHAPTER 15

DAY 3 - FORT SELKIRK

At 3:35am I awoke to the sound of Ardie's voice. I was still feeling well and strong, with the exception of my sunburned, chapped lips. I would use plenty of lip balm the next few days to try and clear up this minor irritation. The morning routine went better today, and we were only about five minutes late. We had entered an area of the Yukon River that has a solid Basalt wall running along the right bank. It was mostly brown, with some shades of white and yellow coloring the different layers of rock. The geologists say this was caused when flowing lava ran into a glacier field eons ago. The walls are close to 100 ft. high. Around 6 am we saw the buildings of historic Fort Selkirk on the left bank.

Archaeology of the Fort Selkirk region has revealed evidence of native peoples going back 10,000 years. This makes it one of the oldest inhabited areas in the New World. Modern history of Fort Selkirk began with the establishment of the Hudson Bay Company Trading Post in 1848.

While I pushed the pace on day one and two, I now felt comfortable getting into a cruising pace that I can sustain for the remainder of the race. If you have the urge to complain about your eight hour work day, think about paddling a canoe for eighteen hours a day. Or better yet, think about doing anything for eighteen hours a day for a week. How did I get through it? I would think in small periods of time. We took a couple of minutes each half hour to eat and drink, so I would think about my choices. Do I want chocolate chip cookies, a trail-mix snack bar or some turkey jerky? Was it time for more sunscreen or aspirin? I also thought about my fellow competitors. They were going through the same thing. This made me more determined to push harder than they were willing to do.

The canoe paddle stroke is very basic. Reach out with the paddle, plant the blade in the water, and pull back. Recover and repeat. Your speed is determined by how much force you put into the effort. Of course some canoe paddle strokes are more efficient than others. It is a grueling, labor intensive activity, but a fast moving river current makes it much more bearable.

Today we had more cloud cover and some wind, so I kept my jacket on a little longer. Shortly after 4 pm. we passed a delta-like area where the White River flows into the Yukon. There were many streams and rivers constantly flowing into the Yukon River, but you definitely noticed the White River. Appropriately named, the river is full of glacier silt and volcanic ash. As it mixes with the greenish waters of the Yukon, it turns the whole river a milky, coffee color. There is so much sediment in the water that if you stopped paddling you could hear the small particles scraping along the canoe. It really ruined the river for me. I wondered how any fish can live in it after this ugly transformation.

Ardie had all the maps, and I was constantly asking him for mileage details. I tried not to be as bad as a child in the back seat of a car asking, "Are we there yet?" But it was another activity to occupy my mind. I figured out that we needed to average 140 miles a day to finish on Sunday. Ardie originally thought we would finish on Monday. This gave us more incentive to keep pushing.

Around 6 pm. we passed the Stewart River and then Stewart Island. We saw a couple of buildings. A trading post was built here in the 1880s. We had hoped to make Dawson City today, but we will fall a little short of that goal. There is a campground there, and if we had made it – the increased human activity probably would have disrupted our camp routine. We found a nice island about 18 miles from Dawson, and set-up our tents. Ardie warmed up some water on his mini-stove, and I had the first of my freeze-dried meals. I picked the beef stroganoff with noodles. It was a good sized meal, and I was sure I couldn't eat it all. Although it was short on beef and long on noodles, I easily finished it off. My hands were starting to get a little rough, so I coated them with vaseline before falling asleep. Ardie estimated we logged another 160 miles today. A Sunday finish was looking even more likely.

DAY FOUR

Ardie and I were now officially over the halfway point. We stopped in Eagle, Alaska to get our passport stamped.

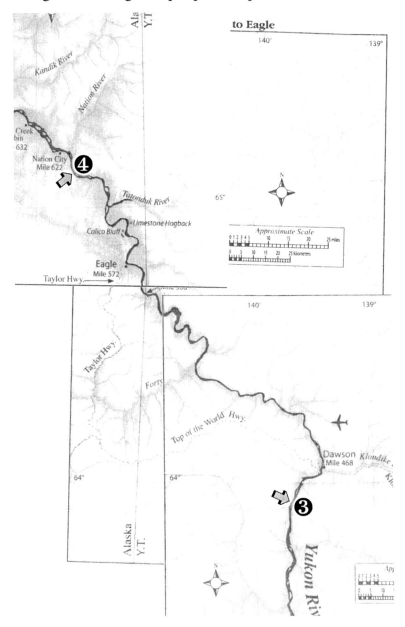

CHAPTER 16

DAY 4 - CROSSING THE BORDER

Thursday morning I woke up a few minutes early, and started breaking camp with a little more energy. It seemed I was adapting to the "sleep a little, paddle all day" routine. Ardie and I hit the water a few minutes past the six-hour minimum. There were two big highlights today. We expected to arrive in Dawson in a little over two hours, and then in the early evening we hoped to make it to Eagle, Alaska – back in the U.S.A.

Dawson is the end of the 460 mile Yukon River Quest held in June, before this race, it was the world's longest canoe and kayak race. Shortly after 7am, we approached Dawson, and spotted Sherry and photographer Ron at a campground on the left bank. We paddled up to the boat ramp, and took about a ten minute break. Sherry gave us updates on the kayaks and voyager team in front of us, but unfortunately no news about how big our lead was over the next canoe. It would have been good to know if our current pace was sufficient to hold our lead. We were soon underway again. Sherry expected to see us again in Eagle.

The river current seemed to increase as we left Dawson. Ardie told me that Eagle is about 100 miles away. I figured we had been averaging around 9 miles per hour the last two days. That meant we should hit Eagle by 8pm. The conditions remained very mild. There is a little cloud cover, and that kept the sun from being too intense. Around noon, we passed the ghost town of Forty Mile, deserted after the gold ran out in the early 1900s. The Forty Mile River flowed into the Yukon, and widened it substantially. Ardie and I were constantly trying to determine where the best current could be found. When the river is over a half-mile wide, you can lose a lot of time going from one side to the other looking for faster water. We generally stayed towards the middle of the river. About 12:30 pm we pulled over to shore, and stretched our legs for about ten minutes. I walked up and down the bank to get the blood pumping to my lower extremities. There was a lot of loose rock and sand on the shore. Closer to the tree-line, we could see many snapped tree trunks that were damaged by large pieces of ice in the Spring thaw.

We were soon back in the canoe heading for Alaska. After several more hours, Ardie informed me that the U.S.A./Canada border was coming up. I expected to see some sort of sign, but the border was very non-descript. No fence, just a ten-foot wide clearing running from the river up the sides of the hills. On the left bank there was a small Canadian and U.S. flag marking the border location. Please don't tell any terrorists about this easy access point to the United States! Ninety minutes later we arrived in the battered township of Eagle. We must stop here to get our passports stamped. I had been concerned that this process could cost us valuable race time. Sherry has the situation under control however, and soon after we hit the shore Officer Collins was there to welcome us back to the U.S.A. and stamp our passports. Pretty cool! How many people enter the U.S. in a canoe (legally)? We said our goodbyes to Sherry. She was picking up an aunt in Fairbanks, so we would not see her again until the finish.

One consequence of entering Alaska was gaining an hour with an earlier time zone. Oh boy! We were able to paddle nineteen hours today instead of eighteen. This information coupled with a pee-bottle mishap that resulted in me sitting in a puddle of my own urine, put me in a "down" mood for an hour or so. But it did not last long, after all – we were leading the Yukon 1000.

A little over an hour after leaving Eagle, we came upon the multi-colored Calico Bluff. The Bluff is made-up of compressed layers of limestone and shale that are seen in contrasting colors of black, yellow, brown and white. I am sure humans have marveled at this sight for thousands of years. It marks the entrance to the Yukon-Charley Rivers National Preserve. We were now officially in Grizzly bear country. Several hours later, we found a suitable island campsite. Ardie and I were getting low on water. Peter Coates, the race organizer, advised us to fill our water jugs when we stopped, and by morning the sediment would have settled to the bottom making it easier to filter. We filled up two water jugs to test the theory. After a somewhat undercooked meal of macaroni and cheese, I was ready for sleep. For the first time, we heard a chorus of howling wolves in the distance. I was too tired to be concerned, and quickly drifted off to sleep. It had been another good day – approximately 167 miles covered.

EAGLE, ALASKA

Eagle, Alaska was founded in 1897 by disgruntled prospectors who left Canada after failing to find gold in the Klondike. The miners, along with a group of businessmen, divided an area bordering the Yukon River into 400 lots. The lots sold for a $5 recording fee, and the new residents were given one year to erect a building. By 1898, the population had reached 700, and Eagle had become a major commercial center for the Upper Yukon. In 1899, the U.S. Army built Ft. Egbert next to the city. The military helped to establish roads and communications in the region. Like Dawson City, Eagle's population dropped after gold was discovered near Fairbanks. In 1911, more residents left when the U.S. Army closed Ft. Egbert.

Today Eagle, known as the "Jewel of the Yukon," has approximately 200 residents. The city has managed to survive while many other gold-boom communities became ghost towns.

Eagle was nearly wiped out in May 2009. Record high temperatures up-river on the Yukon resulted in a rapid ice melt. During the night, ice chunks - some the size of houses, pushed out of the riverbank and damaged or destroyed 25 buildings and many vehicles along Eagle's waterfront. Some of the structures were pushed off their foundations by the massive ice. Estimates are that the water level reached 10 feet above the previous high water mark. Fortunately, everyone survived the calamity.

The real story may be how the townspeople, with the help of private and public resources, have united to rebuild their village before the harsh winter arrives.

DAY FIVE

Ardie and I went to shore in Circle to refill our water jugs. This is as close as we came to seeing any of the towns on land.

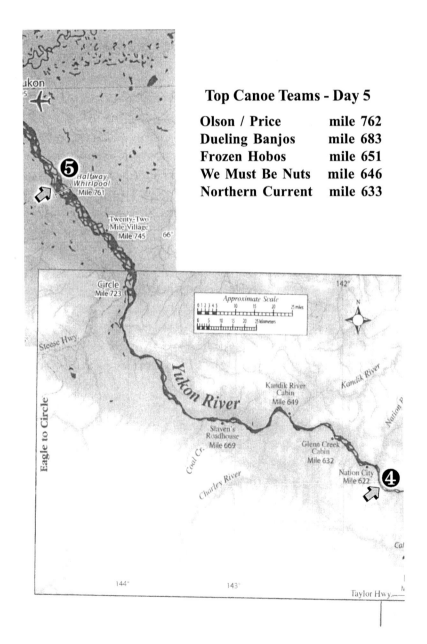

Top Canoe Teams - Day 5

Olson / Price	mile 762
Dueling Banjos	mile 683
Frozen Hobos	mile 651
We Must Be Nuts	mile 646
Northern Current	mile 633

CHAPTER 17

DAY 5 - CIRCLE, ALASKA

I was confident it was now a three day race. Despite Ardie's warnings that our progress would drop in the ominous "Flats" section of the river, our mileage totals over the last three days had put us in a good position to finish on Sunday.

Well, so much for the settling sediment theory. The water in our jugs looked as cloudy as it did five hours ago. This was not a serious problem. If we wanted to take the time, we could find a clear-flowing stream, and filter water from it before it mixed with the Yukon. Ardie and I opted to go ashore in Circle, and see if we could fill our jugs there. We had about 105 miles of paddling to get there. At this point, the Yukon River had grown close to a mile wide. It made the Whitehorse version of the Yukon look like a creek.

Physically, I was still feeling fairly well. I had been applying sports cream to my tight shoulder and neck muscles twice a day. Surprisingly, I did not have any blisters on my hands. It seemed that all of the training sessions had turned our bodies into paddling machines. The biggest challenge for me was occupying the mind. Sometimes the hours would go by quickly, and other times I thought my watch was running backwards.

Today, the hours were passing by steadily. Around 10 am, we passed by Slaven's Roadhouse. Near this site in the early 1900's, a coal mine employing sixty men produced thousands of tons of lignite coal that was delivered to the Dawson Electric Light and Power Company. A few more miles downriver, Ardie saw a Grizzly bear along the shore. We paddled towards it for a closer look, but it ran up the riverbank and into the forest before I could tell how big it was.

We hit Circle about 6 pm, and it was good to get out of the canoe. The long hours of being in a seated position were not good for my legs. Circle was mistakenly named by early surveyors who thought the town was located on the Arctic Circle. It is actually 50 miles south of it. Ardie and I grabbed five empty jugs and walked up the bank. We stopped in a little grocery store, and were told there is drinking water at the "washateria" across the road. Ardie talked me out of buying a tin of canned ham. I guess he was concerned about the extra weight. I headed back to the shore to make sure our canoe was okay while Ardie got the water.

I was curious about a brand new, huge log cabin-type building that it was boarded-up, and looked out of place among the much smaller and older run-down structures in Circle. A local at the boat ramp told me that a company built the two million dollar building anticipating that a ferry would be bringing tourists to stay there. The ferry stopped coming to Circle, and the bank now owned an empty building. Oops!

Ardie soon came back down the bank with the water. I said goodbye to the locals, who were loading their boats for a weekend of fishing, and we were off again. Circle marked the beginning of a crazy 240 mile stretch of the Yukon River known as the "Flats." From maps, the area looked like a braided series of channels that starts to unravel after passing Fort Yukon. A frustrated Ardie put aside the maps, and we tried to read the current in deciding which channel to take. It was not that hard, and we made good progress for the remainder of the day. About 10:30 pm, we pulled up to a good camping spot. Ardie warmed up some water, and I decided on scrambled eggs and bacon for my freeze-dried meal. I added some oatmeal to the mix, and it was very tasty. Our mileage dipped a little today. We covered about 144 miles. Five days completed, and two to go – I hoped.

I would say it was about day five, that the Yukon race exceeded the toughness of the 2009 Everglades Challenge. The sleep deprivation is more immediate in the Everglades race. In the Yukon 1000, we slept for a few hours each night, and we had better water conditions. However, it is not a natural activity to paddle a canoe 18 hours a day, and at some point - our bodies would start to rebel.

DAY SIX

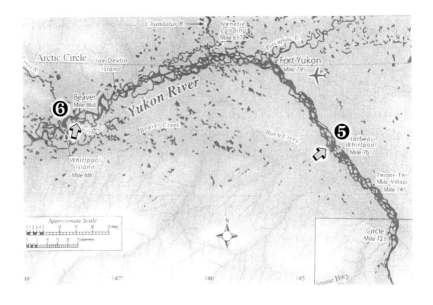

When we reached Ft. Yukon, Ardie and I were paddling a canoe above the Artic Circle dressed in t-shirts and shorts. I was glad we had a big lead. We could have been passed in the Flats area by another team taking a different channel, and would not have known about it until crossing the finish line.

CHAPTER 18

DAY 6 - THE FLATS

As we prepared for our sixth day of paddling on the Yukon River, I was pleased that we were in the 'home stretch" of the race. I figured we had about 220 miles to the finish. Our food and water supplies were fine for two more days.

The first landmark of the day was Fort Yukon, approximately 33 miles away. Thirty minutes into our paddle, I thought I spotted the Voyager team about a mile ahead of us. Another hour went by, and as we came around the bend - they were stopped on the shore. I greeted them with "Ahoy you scalawags!" Brian McDonell, the only crew member I knew, said good morning and asked where we camped last night. Ardie had no idea. The maps were useless since the channels and islands were constantly changing from the different water levels. We had picked up our pace as we went by them. Although they were not in our canoe class, I was hoping to catch them at some point. I was surprised how quickly we pulled away from them. Thirty minutes later, I saw the Voyager come out from a side channel way up ahead of us. So much for catching the Voyager, they obviously had found a great shortcut. Our strategy was to be conservative through the Flats. I was sure there were a few shortcuts to be had, but there were also some channels that may have been blocked by dead trees or could take us miles away from the main channel. It would have been easy for a team to pass us in the flats without us even knowing it. Ardie and I slowly made our way towards Fort Yukon, sometimes making good channel choices and sometimes picking ones' that cost us a little time. Around 10:30 am, we finally passed by Fort Yukon, which was easy to spot with its four or five water towers near the shore. Ardie and I were now above the Arctic Circle. I never thought I would be paddling a canoe in shorts and a t-shirt this far North

Past Fort Yukon, the channel maze of the river became even more complicated as the preferred routes became harder to identify. In one area we were in the main channel when water started gushing towards a smaller channel. Before we could react in time, the current had grabbed us, and we were headed away from our preferred channel. Ardie assured me it would rejoin the main channel, and several miles later it did. As the day progressed, Ardie was able to spot these scenarios, and we avoided being pulled off course. He also was able to identify a couple of shortcuts on the map that worked well for us. Our forward progress had definitely slowed down. Even being in the right channel, we were faced with one long, sweeping turn after another. It had been hazy the last few days as the wind blew smoke from area fires in our direction. This actually helped us by blocking the sunlight, and keeping the temperature a little cooler. During the race, the temperature had usually been between 70 and 80 degrees.

For the most part, mosquitoes and black flies had not been a problem. I did get bit in the back by a black fly when we went to shore in Circle. It was similar to the deer flies we have in Florida, and left a nasty welt after it had its blood meal. Today we were periodically being buzzed by black flies as we paddled. I decided it was payback time, and with keen hand-eye coordination I was able to knock them out of the air with my canoe paddle. At last count I had nine confirmed kills.

We passed the small village of Beaver about 10 pm and found a good camping site a few miles later. Although we had our least productive full day of paddling, Ardie and I should still be able to finish on Sunday. We covered about 110 miles today, and had 110 miles to go. Most importantly, the river conditions would improve as we got closer to the finish. I chose a beef stew packet for my last meal on the river. The potatoes were a little raw, and of course it was light on beef, but I managed to "choke it down." I fell asleep with twitching arm and shoulder muscles, but I had a smile on my face - one more day!"

DAY SEVEN

The Yukon River returned to a single channel and the current increased slightly for the last 18 miles of the race. That helped the final stretch go by quickly. Ardie and I had met our goal of finishing on Sunday, while the rest of the canoe field spent another night on the river.

CHAPTER 19

DAY 7 - THE BEAUTIFUL BRIDGE

I woke up about ten minutes early this morning, and got a head start on breaking down my camp. My neck and shoulder muscles were sore and tight. Where's a masseuse when you need one? Being ahead of schedule, I took out the camera for a few photos. Ardie had gotten a lot of sun on his face, and looked like he fell asleep on a tanning bed. As we loaded the canoe, I bent down to pick up something, and suddenly my neck muscles running along the back of my head seemed to seize up followed immediately by a massive headache. At first, I thought I was having a stroke, but the pain quickly subsided. I took a couple aspirin as a precaution. My body may have been getting tired of the abuse my mind was making it endure.

We were soon moving through the water on the final leg of our journey. Ardie and I were both keeping our break times to a minimum. We were still in the Flats, but it had gotten much easier to stay in the main channel. Our next landmark was Steven's Village, about 84 miles away when we started. It would probably take us over ten hours to get there.

Sleeping just three and a half to four hours each night for a week had caught up to me. Ardie and I had both been experiencing periods of drowsiness the last few days. Ardie had an assortment of caffeinated gels he used to "perk" himself up. I recently started using a five hour liquid energy shot to fight off the "sleep monsters." I took one each of the last two days, and had saved two for today. It was like taking a giant B-12 vitamin, and seemed to have no bad side effects. Ardie said he could tell when I had taken one; our canoe speed picked up and I became more animated. We learned later that the third place kayak team had to pull over for a two-hour nap on the final day. They had run out of caffeine gels, and were about to fall out of their kayak.

Ardie and I were making steady progress towards Steven's Village, and soon could make out some hills in the distance. Around 3:30 pm, we passed the Village and Ardie told me we had only 25 miles to go. Soon the Flats came to an end, and we had one river channel again with hills on each side. The river current increased as we closed in on our goal. The final hours went by quickly, and as we swung around the bend a most magnificent structure appeared - the Alaskan pipeline bridge. Sherry was cheering us on as we crossed the finish line. Our official time was 6 days, 8 hours, and 54 minutes. Ardie and I had won the world's longest canoe race!

Alaska Oil Pipeline

In 1968, a huge oil discovery was made in Prudhoe Bay, Alaska. The problem was getting the oil to market. Every attempt to build a pipeline was blocked by environmental and legal hurdles. The situation changed in 1973 when OPEC initiated an oil embargo against the United States that caused fuel prices to rise sharply. Public outrage pressured Congress to remove all of the challenges that had been blocking the project.

The Alyeska Pipeline Service Company began construction on the pipeline in March of 1975. At its peak, over 28,000 workers were involved in the project. Accidents during the two year project claimed the lives of 31 people. From the North Slope of Alaska to the northern most ice free port in Valdez, Alaska, construction crews ran the pipeline over three mountain ranges and crossed 800 rivers and streams.

The first oil moved through the 800 mile pipeline on June 20, 1977. The total cost was $8 billion in 1977, making it the largest privately financed construction project at the time. The diameter of the pipeline is 48 inches, and the oil travels at 3.7 miles per hour through 11 pump stations. 88,000 barrels flow through the line each hour. As of 2009, over 16 billion barrels have been pumped, and 20,000 oil tankers loaded in Valdez.

Prior to the pipeline's construction in 1976, Alaska was the most heavily taxed state with a 14.5 percent personal income tax. Once the pipeline was finished, the State made billions of dollars from taxes paid by the oil producers and shippers. Alaska abolished it's income tax, and is now the most tax-free state.

The Alaska Oil Pipeline was built to withstand earthquakes and forest fires. It is resistant to gunshots, but not bulletproof. In 2001, Daniel C. Lewis shot a hole through a welded joint in the pipeline, causing a 250,000 gallon oil spill. The oil was cleaned up, and Lewis was sentenced to 16 years in prison for: criminal mischief, assault, drunken driving, oil pollution and misconduct.

If the oil wells run dry and the pipeline stops being used, the Alyeska Company is required by law to remove the pipeline and restore the natural habitat.

CHAPTER 20

Call of the Cheeseburger

Sherry and race organizer, Peter Coates, greeted us as we beached our canoe on the shore below the bridge. Coates congratulated us on winning, and told us how fortunate all of the paddlers were to have had such mild weather conditions. He said on the prior weekend, strong winds were causing eight foot waves under the pipeline bridge. That would have been a miserable way to end the race. We might have been swimming with our canoe across the finish line.

Ardie and I began unloading the canoe, while Sherry backed the SUV down the boat ramp. We were staying at the Yukon River Inn, which was on the Dalton Highway before the pipeline bridge. The Inn was originally built to house construction workers for the oil pipeline project in the 1970s. It is basically a series of connected portable trailers. Each room has two bunk beds, and there is a communal bathroom with multiple shower stalls. In the front of the Yukon Inn is a restaurant that Sherry said was surprisingly good.

I had spent a week on the river without a decent meal or a shower. Which would I choose first? The hot meal of course, although I did change into some clean clothes so I would be less offensive. I ordered a large cheeseburger with fries, and followed that with a slice of blueberry pie and ice cream. I then enjoyed a hot shower in the Inn's rustic bathroom.

The amenities of civilization are much more pleasurable when you have been without them for awhile.

Feeling totally refreshed, I joined Ardie and Sherry back in the restaurant, which was rapidly becoming a lounge area for the finishing paddlers and their support crews. Russ Dawkins and Rob Colliver of the British kayak team, After the Gold Rush, were there. They had finished tied for first with Team Hendron in the kayak class. I listened while Russ spoke about their race. He and his partner had worked-out a detailed race plan covering their stroke rate, food breaks and shore stops. Two days of following their plan resulted in them being close to 20 miles behind the lead kayak. On day three, Dawkins and Colliver picked up their pace and stopped taking any shore breaks. By the end of the day, they had covered 180 miles - the highest daily total of any team in the race. During day five, they caught the two leading kayaks in the Flats. After paddling together for awhile the British trio split up, the team of All the Way 2 took a different channel than the other kayaks. The race was on again, with teams After the Gold Rush and Team Hendron sprinting through the Flats. They continued a strong pace through day six, and did not know if the other kayak was ahead or behind them. That night, Dawkins, Colliver and the Hendron twins agreed to cross the finish line together. On day seven, with each team holding onto the other's kayak, they drifted under the bridge in a time of 6 days, 2 hours, 11 minutes. They were relieved to learn they had finished in first place. The third kayak of Crocker and Hewett came in more than four hours later, after having to stop for an afternoon nap to avoid falling out of the kayak. The voyager canoe finished in fourth place overall in a time of 6 days, 6 hours, 52 minutes. Coates was surprised that the kayaks turned in the fastest times. He thought the voyager team would be the quickest.

We soon wrapped up the "chat" session, and I was ready for another amenity that we all take for granted -sleeping in a real bed. Ardie and I were pleased not to be spending another night on the river like the rest of the canoe racers who were still miles from the finish. It was very satisfying to know that all of our hours of planning and training had culminated in victory.

Monday morning Ardie, Sherry and their aunt decided to do some sightseeing in the area. I opted to sleep-in, and wait for some of the other canoe teams to finish. Shortly after 11 am, the second place canoe team, Dueling Banjos, arrived. At 21 and 22 years old, Josia Freeman and Ben Couturier were the youngest participants in the race. Both Alaskan natives, they entered the race without any preparation. Freeman and Couturier borrowed a friend's wooden canoe, and made a spray skirt for it the night before the race. Although Ardie and I had a 90 mile lead on them after day four, the Alaskan lads seemed to be getting stronger. Their combined mileage totals for days five, six and seven were higher than any other team. They were surprised that a couple of "old guys" had beaten them.

Eight hours later, another team of Alaskans, Jonathan Morgan and Ben Schmidt, the Frozen Hobos, crossed under the bridge. From 10:30 to 11:30 pm, four more canoe teams avoided another night of camping. Among them was the first co-ed team of Brenda Forsythe, 51, and Larry Seethaler, 66 - team We Must be Nuts. Larry's partner dropped out a week before the competition, and Brenda decided to join her husband in the epic race. Amazingly, they were still smiling and talking to each other as they came ashore. Brenda and Larry are both professors at the University of Alaska.

It would be ten days before the last canoe completed the race. All of the competitors in the Yukon 1000 have my respect. I know many serious canoe and kayak racers who would be scared to death to enter an event of this magnitude. For me, the Yukon 1000 had the perfect mix of adventure, endurance and competition.

Achievement Validates Existence

The movie, "300," is based on actual events that happened in the Battle of Thermopylae in 480 BC. In that battle, three hundred Spartans and their allies held a mountain pass for three days against the overwhelming onslaught of King Xerxes million-man force. The Spartans' sacrifice gave Sparta and the other Greek city-states enough time to ready their armies, and ultimately drive the Persians out of Greece.

There is a scene in "300," where a Spartan soldier, upon seeing the massive Persian army stretching into the horizon, is excited about facing them in battle. The Spartan says he has waited his whole life to go up against a worthy foe. That is much the same feeling the Yukon 1000 provided for me. After competing in hundreds of races over three decades, my "worthy foe" was waiting for me in Canada and Alaska.

In Whitehorse, as I stood on the shore of the Yukon River with the other competitors, and carefully loaded my canoe with supplies and gear before the race, our whole group reminded me of a Spartan regiment going into battle. Surely, people like these, who push their mental and physical limitations in extreme adventure races are the modern Spartans of our society. Just as the ancient Spartans were taught to endure pain and hardship without complaint, so too would these weekend warriors. I felt a strong sense of comradeship with the Yukon racers. While we were competing against each other, the true prize was completing the challenge.

When I was competing in my twenties, I remembered seeing a few sixty and seventy year old competitors, and wondered what motivated them to race. Now that I have reached the half century mark, I have an understanding of their desire. It can take a long time to figure out how to spend a relatively short life. When you finally discover your life's passion - why would you ever want to give it up?

So returning to the question of why I spend countless hours and considerable amounts of money engaging in harsh competitions with very little public or financial recognition, my answer has become my life's motto - "Achievement Validates Existence." If you are not striving to accomplish goals in your life, what is the point of being here? For me, achievement is how I validate my existence.

RESULTS OF THE 2009 YUKON 1000 INAUGURAL
WORLD'S LONGEST CANOE AND KAYAK RACE

TEAM # & CLASS	TEAM NAME	RACERS & AGE	COUNTRY OF ORIGIN	FINISH TIME
04 Kayak	Team Hendron	R. Hendron, 27	London, UK	06:02:11
		H. Hendron, 27	Surrey, UK	
15 Kayak	After the	R. Colliver, 44	Hamshire, UK	06:02:11
	Goldrush	R. Dawkins, 43	London, UK	
01 Kayak	All the Way 2	D. Crocker, 39	Berkshire, UK	06:06:30
		E. Hewett, 44	Berkshire, UK	
10 Voyager Class Canoe	Yukon Voyager	K. Newell, 62	NY., USA	06:06:52
		P. Repak, 58	NY., USA	
		H. Crouch, 51	NY., USA	
		M. Trump, 26	PA, USA	
		M. Trump, 24	PA, USA	
		T. Stout, 55	PA, USA	
		B. McDonnell, 50	NY, USA	
11 Canoe	Price / Olson	Rod Price, 49	FL, USA	06:08:54
		Ardie Olson, 47	GA, USA	
19 Canoe	Dueling Banjos	B. Couturier, 22	AK, USA	07:00:18
		J. Freeman, 21	AK, USA	
14 Canoe	Frozen Hobos	J. Morgan, 29	AK, USA	07:08:07
		B. Schmidt, 31	AK, USA	
08 Canoe	Yukon Duet	B. Carrigan, 50	MN, USA	07:11:27
		R. Ring-Jarvi, 59	MN, USA	
07 Canoe	We Must Be Nuts	B. Forsythe, 51	AK, USA	07:11:55
		L. Seethaler, 66	AK, USA	
18 Canoe	Tim X Two	T. van Nest, 62	MI, USA	07:12:32
		T. van Nest, Jr., 45	AK, USA	
03 Canoe	Northern Current	A. McLain, 35	AK, USA	07:12:34
		C. McLain, 35	AK, USA	
05 Kayak	Humpbacks	S. Daigle, 48	AK, USA	08:00:00
		M. Sullivan, 28	AK, USA	
09 Canoe	Best of the Mediocre	D. Berg, 65	MN, USA	08:00:03
		D. Dahl, 59	MN, USA	
06 Canoe	Gonzos	A. Billiard, 59	NS, CAN	09:00:07
		NG. Warnica, 63	NS, CAN	
16 Canoe	Tanned, Rested and Ready	T. Herbst, 38	ID, USA	10:00:04
		B. Polk, 43	ID, USA	
02 Canoe	Fruit Loops	J. Ders, 60	NY, USA	DNF
		M. Houck, 47	NY, USA	
17 Canoe	The Aching Joints	B. Lee, 59	AK, USA	DNF
		J. Lee, 61	AK, USA	

ABOUT THE AUTHOR

Now where was that checkpoint?

Rod Price lives on his own terms in Orlando, FL. He owns and operates an office products company in Central Florida. This allows him to train for his adventure races in the mornings. While many adults are slowing down in their forties, Rod had the most adventure filled decade of his life.

Born in South Carolina, Rod moved to Central Florida with his family in 1973. He went to community college in Leesburg, FL on a tennis scholarship. Rod spent four years in the Washington, D.C. area working for a U.S. Senator while attending college at the University of Maryland with a major in journalism.

Rod has one daughter, Chelsea, who is currently a sophomore at Florida State University. Chelsea has been a frequent helper in the business, and at her father's races.

Protecting the natural habitat is important to Rod. He devotes his charitable time to the Friends of the Wekiva River, a Central Florida organization whose mission is to safeguard the Wekiva River Basin northwest of Orlando. Rod serves as a board member, and organizes a yearly canoe and kayak race for the group.

In addition to coordinating adventure racing clinics, Rod has enjoyed speaking to organizations and corporate clients about the benefits of adventure racing for teamwork building, assessing strengths and weaknesses and overcoming perceived personal limitations.

Rod can be contacted at his adventure racing website – www.RodPriceAdventure.com

World's Longest Canoe Race 2009 Yukon 1000

Whitehorse to the Alaska Pipeline — 1000 Miles 1600 Km

Yukon 1000
2009
World's Longest Canoe Race

Ardie packs his bear canister with food.

Paddlers Pre-Race Meeting

Preparing the mental game and checking weather conditions.

Packing canoes for the Yukon 1000

We made a practice run in our Jensen canoe.

Bluff approaching the Five Finger Rapids

Voyager canoe manages the Five Finger Rapids

One of the formations that gives the
rapids its name, Five Fingers Rapids

Choosing our path through the whitewater

Ardie and I have an exciting run through the Five Finger Rapids.

Until you see it from a canoe you can never
imagine the vastness of the Yukon Territory

Coming ashore at Dawson City, Yukon Territory, Canada

Two of the Bristish Kayak Teams

An aerial view of one of the many bluffs
on our journey down the Yukon River

Saying hello to Sherry, Ardie's wife, at Carmacks who was an excellent "support crew" and morale booster at various stages of the race.

The historic Whitehorse—Dawson Road was a
vital link between the two communities.

A speeding ticket? No, just Officer Collins
stamping my passport as we enter the United
States by water at Eagle, Alaska.

We are just a little speck on the mighty Yukon
as you can see in these pictures.

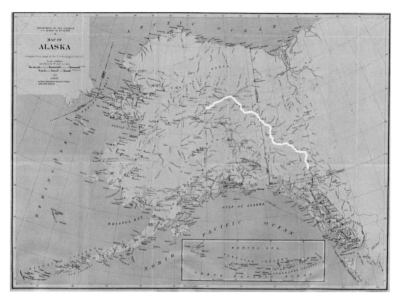

Yellow line shows the route we traveled across
the Yukon territory from Canada to Alaska.

A Google satellite view of the Flats shows how
tricky choosing the right channel can be.

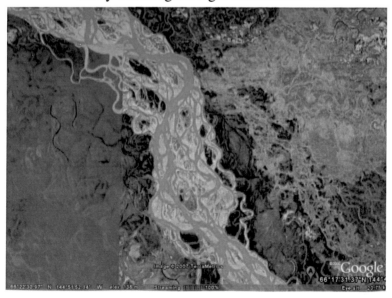

Ardie liked setting his tent on the gravel
while I preferred the smooth sand.

I was proud to be paddling in a Jensen designed canoe.

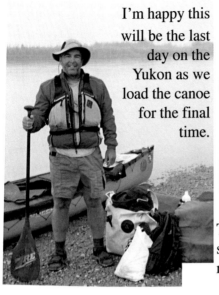

I'm happy this will be the last day on the Yukon as we load the canoe for the final time.

Ardie smiles through the pain.

The morning of the last day shows the physical toll this race was taking on me.

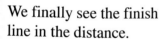

We finally see the finish line in the distance.

The Dalton Highway Pipeline Bridge can be seen through the smoky haze from the wildfires in the area.

We pass under the Pipeline Bridge, Hallelujah!

Ardie and I are awarded our First Place medals in the Canoe Class from Peter Coates, race organizer.

The Yukon 1000 medal represents more mileage
than all the trophies combined in this case.

"Achievement Validates Existence"
— Rod Price